What People Are Saying A

In Volume 2, Steve guides us throug
well as using Reiki for specific physi   ..... ne expands on
many more techniques for healing with Reiki and gives step-by-step
instructions. This is a wonderful addition to the first volume and
helps to understand chakras at an eye-opening level, making this
and the concept of Reiki more understandable and so much more
accessible to everyone. Both of these books are clear, concise, and
make one feel at ease with learning and using Reiki. Also, I highly
recommend the attunements series! *SM*

I really love this book. It is really great to see someone open up in
this selfless way to offer what is rightfully ours as humans, a way to
heal ourselves. The world can use as much love as it can get. Reiki
was meant to be free, not only for the wealthy, or to make people
wealthy. Yes, I believe that a person's time and effort should be
rewarded by an exchange of energy, but $10,000 is way beyond. It is
like charging money for air. *SS*

I purchased all of Steve Murray's attunements for Reiki 1, 2, and 3,
plus his books, and all have been wonderful. I have had wonderful
spiritual awakenings and have healed myself along with helping
others both locally and long distance. I have even astral-traveled
several times and have had others say when I send long distance
to them they are floating or see visions. Once I had a person astral-
travel with me while channeling Reiki to them. I recommend Steve's
attunements very highly and also his books and music. Thank you,
Steve, for making these available to those of us who cannot receive
these attunements in other ways. *BBH*

No holds barred, this book tells all. When I first took Reiki there were
many secrets that weren't ever supposed to be discussed with others
who were not attuned. I mean, there was stuff taught that you're not
supposed to share with others until they pay and take the class, so I
understand how this book must have shocked many Reiki Masters. It
shows the secret Reiki Symbols and how to use them. And you know
what? I think it's time to share the powers of this healing technique
with anyone and everyone who wants/needs it, and it should be
taught at an affordable price. This book does all that. *WH*

1

This book comes with me wherever I go. It's a great quick reference guide for the symbols, how to give an attunement, and answers any questions you may have. After reading this book, I was able to give myself Reiki with a renewed belief and spirit. After purchasing this book, I purchased Steve's DVDs. I highly recommend all of the Reiki programs Steve Murray has to offer. They are awe-inspiring. *JS*

The beauty of this book is its simplicity. Any practitioner of any degree can use this attunement and it does work. As a Reiki Master, I will be recommending this book to all of my students. My hat is off to Steve Murray! Thank you for making your knowledge public!!! Can't wait until the next book comes out. *DZ*

I just finished reading this book and I love it! I knew very little about chakras before I read this book, but the information given was very informative. Steve did a great job of getting all of the major, important facts in there and it has helped me a lot! Another fantastic piece of work! Can't wait for the next one! *BM*

Whether you're curious about Reiki, have been attuned to Reiki, or are a Reiki practitioner, these books are a "must have" in your collection. Both are packed with everything you need to know or should know about Reiki. They also contain a lot of extra information so that you're sure to be left satisfied. *RM*

Compared to the other books I have purchased, this one is the best, and most valuable. Other books merely "talk" about Reiki and attunements instead of explaining them. I remember having many questions about Reiki and not being able to find the answers. Ever since I got this book I've been very pleased, and so have others who have borrowed it from me. *HD*

I recommend this book to all who are reaching for the ultimate knowledge of self-awareness, unconditional love, and spiritually seeking their purpose. Best of all, with this book, you are able to teach, share, and work with others to experience Reiki. *RS*

Reiki

The Ultimate Guide Vol. 3
Learn New Reiki Aura Attunements
Heal Mental & Emotional Issues

S t e v e   M u r r a y

First Printing

Body & Mind Productions, Inc.

Reiki
The Ultimate Guide Vol. 3
Learn New Reiki Aura Attunements
Heal Mental & Emotional Issues

Published by
Body & Mind Productions
820 Bow Creek Lane, Las Vegas, NV 89134
Website: www.healingreiki.com
Email: bodymindheal@aol.com

First Printing March 2006

Library of Congress Cataloging-in-Publication Data
Murray, Steve
The Reiki Ultimate Guide Vol. 3 Learn New Reiki Aura Attunements
Heal Mental & Emotional Issues
/ Murray, Steve – 1st ed.
Library of Congress Control Number 2005906630
ISBN # 0-9771609-1-2
Includes bibliographical references and index.
1. Reiki 2. New Age 3.Alternative Health
4. Self-Healing 5. Spiritual 6. Healing

Cover design: Alan Berrelleza, armb-design@cox.net
Type design, production and photography: Alan Berrelleza
Editors: Sonya Baity, Carol von Raesfeld
Drawings: Mike Zug

Printed in U.S.A.

DVDs-CDs-BOOKS

BOOKS BY STEVE MURRAY

Reiki The Ultimate Guide
Learn Sacred Symbols and Attunements
Plus Reiki Secrets You Should Know

Reiki The Ultimate Guide Vol. 2
Learn Reiki Healing with Chakras
plus New Reiki Healing Attunements
for All Levels

Reiki The Ultimate Guide Vol. 3
Learn New Reiki Aura Attunements
Heal Mental and Emotional Issues

Cancer Guided Imagery Program
For Radiation, Chemotherapy, Surgery
and Recovery

Stop Eating Junk!
In 5 Minutes a Day for 21 Days

DVDS BY STEVE MURRAY

Reiki Master Attunement
Become a Reiki Master

Reiki 1st Level Attunement
Give Healing Energy to Yourself
and Others

Reiki 2nd Level Attunement
Learn and Use the Reiki Sacred
Symbols

Reiki Psychic Attunement
Open and Expand Your Psychic
Abilities

Reiki Healing Attunement
Heal Emotional-Mental Physical-
Spiritual Issues

Lose Fat and Weight
Stop Eating Junk!
In 5 Minutes a Day for 21 Days

Cancer Guided Imagery
Program for Radiation

Cancer Guided Imagery
Program for Chemotherapy

Cancer Guided Imagery
Program for Surgery

30-Day Subliminal
Weight Loss Program

Pain Relief Using Your
Unconscious Mind
A Subliminal Program

Fear & Stress Relief
Using Your Unconscious Mind
A Subliminal Program

Stop Smoking Using Your
Unconscious Mind
A Subliminal Program

5

CDs BY STEVE MURRAY

Reiki Healing Music
Attunement: Volume One

Reiki Healing Music
Attunement: Volume Two

Reiki Psychic Music
Attunement: Volume One

Reiki Psychic Music
Attunement: Volume Two

Cancer Fear & Stress Relief Program
Reduce Fear and Stress During Cancer
Treatment and Recovery

DVDs BY BODY & MIND PRODUCTIONS

Learning to Read the Tarot
Intuitively

Learning to Read the Symbolism
of the Tarot

This Guide is Dedicated to

Wei, Norma, and Joe Murray

Foreword

Reiki and Healing is discussed in my previous Reiki books, but it is important to mention it now for the first-time reader of my books, and to reiterate for all my previous readers.

The key to a healthy life while we are on our earthly journey is a holistic balance in all aspects of our lives. Unfortunately, it is the human condition that all of us will experience ill health -- physically, mentally, or emotionally – at one time or another. The key is to keep it to a minimum and when it does occur, to use a balanced approach to healing.

I believe in the benefits of the Eastern Philosophy of Preventive Medicine to remain healthy on all levels, and I practice it. I have been extremely successful with this philosophy in my life. I also believe in the power and technology of Western Medicine in healing, and would not hesitate to use it if needed; although, I would take responsibility for myself and research Western medications and/or treatments before I proceeded with them. I would combine Reiki with any treatment(s) I decided upon.

Miracles can and do happen using only Reiki or prayers or Western Medicine, etc., but, usually in a successful healing, there are no shortcuts. It's a balanced process with a treatment plan that's best for the circumstances. I believe that plan includes Reiki, other healing modalities, perseverance, and patience.

So, having said that, it is important to understand that Aura Attunements are not a substitute for professional medical care or any condition requiring immediate medical attention. With any mental and emotional issues, Reiki should be used in conjunction with professional medical treatment instead of by itself. Depending on the mental or emotional issue, treatments can include conventional medical doctors and/or one or more other medical practitioners such as a naturopath, osteopath, chiropractor, hypnotherapist, acupuncturist, dietician, etc., whichever you determine is appropriate for your circumstances.

Reiki as an adjunctive therapy can be a very effective and an important element of a healing program. For example, if you break your arm, you should go to the doctor to have it set and put into a cast, then channel Reiki to the arm so it can heal faster. You would not expect Reiki to set the bone.

I understand that the above might be obvious for most people, but I do receive e-mails from people stating that after taking years to become ill or being ill for many years and not addressing the problem, they expect to receive a few Reiki Attunements and become healed. It does not work that way. Usually becoming sick is a process and becoming well is a process. Using Reiki, or any healing modality, Western Medicine, pills and drugs are not going to heal you instantly. I do believe if you include Reiki Attunements with other healing modalities the majority of the time, the healing process will become easier and quicker.

Since everyone's life journey and circumstances are different and unique, concerning mental and emotional issues, it can be a few days to a few weeks or a month before any changes are experienced or felt after receiving an Aura Attunement. The key to a successful outcome is to be consistent with the Aura Attunements and all other treatments prescribed for the mental and emotional issues, and most of all, have patience.

Every person's life journey and circumstances are different. Throw in life's big picture on top of that and it's impossible for any Healer to figure out or understand why Reiki does not help at all times.

I have heard many reasons why Reiki sometimes does not heal and I assume some are correct at times. They include, "it is too late for the physical body to heal" or "it's the person's Karma not to heal." Another is, "since metaphysical laws state if a person does not desire healing, either unconsciously or consciously, it can be rejected."

I believe Healers should never make judgments on whether Reiki is not healing or give a reason why it is not healing any person, even if they believe it is one of the reasons I mentioned. The reality is nobody really knows why Reiki does not work at times, but, most importantly, I believe a Healer should never give up unless told to do so.

Steve Murray

CONTENTS

Specific Reiki Aura Attunements - 137

A Few Notes To My Readers

Throughout this book I will assume you have read the first two books in my Reiki Ultimate Guide trilogy, but in case you have not, I will insert certain content from the previous books where I feel it is needed to help you understand the teachings in this book. If you have not yet read them, I highly recommend that you obtain the other two Reiki books so that you will have access to my complete teachings on Reiki Healing and Reiki Attunements.

In this book I do show how all levels can perform Reiki Aura Attunements, but if you are only a Reiki First Level Healer, you should receive the Reiki Second Level Attunement as soon as possible as it will enable you to use the Reiki Mental and Emotional Symbol when you perform Reiki Aura Attunements.

I have been asked why I do not include any history of Reiki in my books. The first and most important reason is the available space I have in my books. I want to use as much of the space I am allowed to convey as much information as Reiki Healers can actually use in their sessions, so I leave the history telling to others. There are many good books about Reiki history, and other books include some history in their content, so you are not lacking resources on Reiki history. I have included a few books in my bibliography that contain Reiki history.

However, I must say I have become very uncomfortable with the way Reiki history has become very subjective and politicized. Add to this the fact that Reiki history has changed over the years, so as new information is uncovered, a certain percent of Reiki history books have become outdated and are incorrect.

In closing, I believe that my being open and honest with Reiki in all my books and DVD programs will encourage people to embrace Reiki and become Reiki Healers - which is the foundation of my Reiki Mission Statement.

My Reiki Mission Statement

To make Reiki knowledge, guidance, and Attunements available to everyone who seeks them. To make Reiki First, Second, and Master Level Attunements affordable for everyone so that healing can be spread throughout the world.

You cannot open a book without learning something.

-Confucius

Reiki
Ultimate Healing Toolbox

Healing Wheel

**The expectations of life depend upon diligence;
the mechanic that would perfect his work
must first sharpen his tools.**

-Confucius

The Tool Box

Y̶ou have in your hands my final book in the Reiki Ultimate Guide trilogy. Now, with all three Reiki books complete, together they comprise the Reiki Ultimate Healing Toolbox. I believe this Reiki Healing toolbox will inform and empower you with options for all healing situations -- mental, emotional, physical, and spiritual.

The Reiki Healing guidance in this toolbox can be used when you perform Reiki Healing or Attunements on yourself, relatives, friends, and clients, or if you decide to become a Reiki Teacher. You can use the guidance that resonates with you and with which you feel comfortable, and leave the rest in the Reiki Healing toolbox where it might be needed in the future.

Before I go forward, let me give a brief overview of the first two Reiki books so that the first two paragraphs above can be put into context.

First Two Books

The first book in the Reiki trilogy, *Reiki The Ultimate Guide, Learn Sacred Symbols and Attunements Plus Reiki Secrets You Should Know*, gives information on Reiki Healing that is not usually provided or explained to Reiki students, Reiki information seekers, and/or even Reiki Masters. The book helps to fill in the knowledge gaps these people have about Reiki and tells why this information is difficult to obtain.

The book also explains and shows the Reiki Symbols and how to use them. It includes instructions with step-by-step photos that demonstrate how to perform all the Reiki Level Attunements, from 1st Level to Reiki Master, including the Reiki Psychic and Healing Attunements.

Showing and explaining the Reiki Attunements in print caused a bit of controversy at first (and still does to this day) among some Reiki healers who believe everything about Reiki should be kept secret until they decide the circumstances under which it can be divulged. The circumstances usually include the payment of money, (sometimes large sums of it), which denies and/or keeps many people from experiencing Reiki. In my book, I state the reasons why I do not believe in keeping any Reiki secrets, specifically my regard for Reiki as an unconditional healing practice.

The second book is *Reiki The Ultimate Guide Vol. 2, Learn Reiki Healing with Chakras plus New Reiki Healing Attunements for All levels*. Volume 2 explains in detail Reiki Healing with Chakras and presents a formula for New Reiki Healing Attunements using the Chakras for all physical ailments and diseases.

The book also includes illustrations, diagrams, and step-by-step photos to make it easy to learn and perform the Reiki Healing Attunements. This second book did resonate in a positive manner, even with critics of my first book, because of the options it gives them with healing for all physical ailments and diseases, and also the fact that these Attunements can be performed in 15 minutes or less.

Both books became very popular in the Reiki genre around the world soon after they were published. They are instrumental in helping me continue to meet my goal of making Reiki information and guidance available to all who seek it.

Final Book

In this book, the final one in the Reiki trilogy, you will learn about the Aura and the layers within it. Most importantly, however, you will learn how to perform Attunements[1] in the Aura for specific mental and emotional issues, which I call "Reiki Aura Attunements."

Just as in the two previous Reiki books, I convey the information as simply as I can and keep it straightforward and concise so it is easy to read and understand.

Okay, let's start the teachings.

---

[1]An Attunement is a sacred process, initiation, and/or meditation with a specific purpose and intent. A spiritual master performs it.

Aura

Healing Wheel

The object of the superior man is truth.
-Confucius

Aura Defined

two

Before we begin, I need to mention that there are many teachings and much literature that exists with regard to interpretations of the Aura, and some may differ from mine. If you find that in some areas your Aura teachings are diverse from mine, do not worry about it. All Aura teachings do agree on one point -- that there is a mental and emotional energy field that exists outside the physical body. As you will discover later on in this book, these two fields are very important when performing Reiki Aura Attunements.

Aura History

The awareness of an energy field around us has existed throughout civilizations for thousands of years to the present day. Ancient Hindus, Buddhists, Greeks, and Romans depicted energy fields in old paintings, art of significant people and Gods. You also have the halo that is reflected in the art of Christian saints throughout history to the present day. This energy field surrounding the physical body is now commonly called the Aura.

From Buddhist priests to Native American shamans, many spiritual leaders of various doctrines throughout history have incorporated these energy fields (Auras) in their religious and healing rituals, and healing modalities. Today, there are many books* and teachings on the subject of Auras.

Aura

Aura is a Latin word meaning "Light" or "Glow of Light." The Webster's New World Dictionary definition of an Aura is "an invisible emanation or vapor" or "a particular atmosphere or quality that seems to arise from and surround a person or thing."

---

* I list a few in the Bibliography at the back of this book.

28

The most common scientific belief is that the Aura is a subtle energy field surrounding the human body created by molecules, atoms, and cells. As these elements interact and coexist, they create this subtle, magnetic, multi-dimensional energy field. Having said that, the following are my beliefs on the Aura.

My Aura Beliefs

◆ The Aura is much more than just a simple magnetic field surrounding your physical body; rather, it is a very complex system that is part of your very essence, which we have yet to fully understand.

◆ Your Aura and your physical body are the complete you, all one unit. You cannot have one without the other.

◆ Your Aura and your body communicate and exchange information that you need to exist and navigate in your physical life. This is done during every moment, awake or asleep, consciously or unconsciously.

◆ Our Auras contain the complete blueprints for our lives. Our consciousness and all our thoughts, feelings, and even awareness are integrated with and also stored in the Aura.

◆ The Aura contains all of our individual life experiences from the moment we are born until the moment we die. These life experiences (memories) are carried forward and reincarnated in future physical lives.

◆ The Aura reflects our health -- physically, mentally, emotionally, and spiritually. It also reflects our mental and emotional activity.

◆ The Aura is where a majority of mental and emotional issues can start. If these issues are not resolved, they eventually resonate down to the physical body and manifest as symptoms of an illness or a disease.

◆ The Aura can also show disease and ailments in the physical body before any symptoms have manifested there.

◆ One of the main sources of communication from the physical body to the Aura and the Aura back to the physical body are the Chakras.

◆ All living things -- flowers, trees, animals, fish, and so forth -- have an Aura, although not as complex as the Human Aura.

Shape-Size-Color

Most Human Auras extend from the body about five feet, although with more spiritually evolved and developed individuals, Auras can extend outward perhaps seven feet or more.

People who can fully see the entire Aura describe it as an egg shape or bubble of spiritual light, consisting of a haze radiating all around the physical body and shimmering with light and all color combinations.

Aura Layers

I believe the Human Aura is a composite of seven layers (Fig.1) surrounding the physical body. Some teachings describe more layers, but most will include a variation of these seven layers.

These layers are also called "auric layers, subtle bodies, energy fields, energy bodies, or bodies." Throughout this book I will use the term "layer."

Each layer relates to the physical, mental, emotional, and spiritual aspects of the person. Each layer consists of vibrating energy frequencies which can change, depending on the state of the layer. These states will depend on the physical, mental, emotional, and spiritual conditions of the person and the circumstances they are experiencing at any given moment.

All seven layers occupy the same space surrounding each other in successive layers, with each layer extending out beyond the last.

The layers are interconnected and reliant on the other layers for their normal function. At the same time, all layers function interactively with the physical body at some level.

The first three layers interface with material or physical needs of the body and also relate to the mind, ideas, emotions, health, and desires. The fourth layer acts as a buffer and intermediary between the others. These four layers are the ones you will use with the Aura Attunement. The outer three layers interface and relate with your spiritual needs, your soul, and spirit.

In the next chapter, I will discuss each of the Seven Layers of the Aura.

All Auras

(Fig.1) Seven Layers of the Aura with the Seven Chakras

A journey of a thousand miles
begins with a single step.

-Confucius

Seven Layers

Yͦou are not just a physical body with an Aura surrounding you. You are an Aura with a physical body and both together comprise one complete being. As I mentioned before, you cannot have one without the other. So let's talk about the physical body first before I describe the Seven Layers of the Aura.

Physical Body

The physical body (Fig. 2) is the most tangible part of our being. It provides stability and a solid foundation for the Aura. It helps us, in the here and now, to be conscious of our environment, to walk, talk, eat, etc. It is our vehicle of transportation for our journey through life.

The physical body is also an ongoing barometer on how healthy and balanced you are during your journey in this life, although this physical barometer sometimes does not reflect in real time your state of health. For example, if you cut your finger, you know your state of health immediately, but if you have emotional or mental issues that are not being addressed, symptoms will eventually manifest in your physical body in the future. The good news is that with the information (symptoms) you receive from your physical body, you can make the necessary changes or adjustments needed to stay in a healthy, balanced state in both your Aura and physical body.

The physical body has the Chakras[2], and by this time in your learning process, you know of their importance in your healing work. But the physical body also has the brain, which functions, in part, as a medium or relay switch to translate and process emotional and mental information coming and going throughout your complete being.

---

[2]Sanskrit word meaning "spinning wheel" used in reference to each of the seven major energy centers in the physical body.

Physical Body

Fig.2   Physical Body

Seven Layers of the Aura

Etheric Layer

The first layer is the Etheric Layer (Fig.3). Ether refers to a state between energy and matter. This layer extends up to two inches away from the body. Being the first layer closest to the body, it fits like a second skin and is in constant motion.

This layer is the map or blueprint for the physical body. It holds impressions of all the organs, glands, Chakras, and Meridians. It is where the Reiki can be felt or sensed as it flows through Meridians and Chakras. Physical signs of illness and injury can also be detected in this layer by scanning[3], a process at which experienced Reiki Healers excel. Blockages with Reiki in the Meridians and Chakras can also be detected in this layer by scanning.

People who can see this layer say it usually appears as shades of blue or gray right near the skin. The shade of the blue or gray relates to the condition and health of the physical body.

Emotional Layer

The second layer is the Emotional Layer (Fig.4) and it extends about two to four inches away from the physical body. The Emotional Layer is a swirling mass of energy that reflects the feelings and emotions we have and experience. It is always in a state of flux

---

[3]When Healers pass hand(s) over physical body to determine problem areas.

Etheric Layer

(Fig.3) Etheric Layer

Emotional Layer

(Fig.4) Emotional Layer

because our emotions and feelings are constantly changing due to our circumstances in life and how we perceive them. The layer loosely resembles the human shape, but is not as defined as the Etheric Layer.

All emotions -- happiness, hope, love, anger, sorrow, hate -- are in this layer. It also stores all unresolved emotions, including fear, resentment, anger, loneliness, and so forth. The state of the Emotional Layer affects the Etheric Layer, which in turn affects the physical body. The Emotional Layer expresses the state of the Mental Layer, which is the next layer out.

People who can see this layer describe all the colors in the rainbow, with positive emotions creating bright colors and negative feelings creating dark colors.

Mental Layer

The third layer is the Mental Layer (Fig.5) and extends about four to eight inches away from the physical body. This layer contains our thoughts, ideas, beliefs, logic, and intellect. It also contains our mental processes and reflects the conscious mind at any moment. In this layer, thought and ideas are formulated and authenticated. Mental health and/or mental issues are also reflected here.

The Mental Layer's information resonates down to the emotional body, which reacts to it with your programmed emotional responses. However, these programmed emotional responses to situations and circumstances can be changed, and sometimes must be changed for a healthy

Mental Layer

(Fig.5) Mental Layer

physical state to be possible. Reiki Aura Attunements can help with this.

People who can see this layer describe the color as a bright shade of yellow that becomes brighter when a person is focusing on a mental process.

Astral Layer

The Astral Layer (Fig.6) is the fourth layer and it extends about eight to twelve inches away from the physical body. This layer separates the first three layers from the outer three layers. The Astral Layer is the bridge or portal between the physical world and the spiritual world. The connection to the physical world is your body and the first three Aura Layers. This is an important layer in performing Reiki Aura Attunements and you will learn to work within it. The connection to the spiritual world is the next three layers beyond the Astral Layer.

People who can see the Astral Layer state it is a brightly colored rainbow with a rosy hue.

The next three layers are where the definitions are more esoteric and interpretations are very subjective from various teachings. I believe these layers can expand with evolving spiritual awareness.

Astral Layer

Fig.6 Astral Layer

Etheric Template Layer

The fifth layer is the Etheric Template Layer (Fig.7) and it extends about one to two feet away from the physical body. Its primary function is to keep the Etheric Layer (first layer) in place and it contains a template of the physical body on a higher spiritual level. This layer also contains your unique inner identity, the essence of your present state of being, and all the possible futures on your physical plane.

The most common perception of this color is a dark blue or cobalt blue.

Celestial Layer

The sixth layer is the Celestial Layer (Fig.8). It extends about two to three feet away from the body. The Celestial Layer reflects the subconscious mind. It is the layer where we can experience unconditional love and spiritual ecstasy. It's the layer of feelings within the world of our spirit, the layer of emotions on the spiritual plane. Group consciousness and universal love are here.

The Celestial Layer, when perceived, is described as a bright, shimmering light, composed mostly of pastel colors.

Ketheric Layer

The seventh layer is the Ketheric Layer (Fig.9) and it extends about three to five feet away from the body depending on your spiritual state, although it can expand as your spirituality awareness increases. The energies in this layer spin at the highest frequency of all the layers.

45

People who can see or sense this layer say its spin forms an oval similar to an egg, which surrounds and protects everything within it. With developed spiritual awareness, this form changes to more of a circle. It is believed this layer can become a perfect circle when a person achieves their highest spiritual awareness. Such a level of awareness is achieved by only a very few individuals.

This is the ultimate layer that is immortal, all knowing, and through this layer we can become one with our source. It is our spiritual template. Through this layer the soul communicates with the conscious mind via the subconscious mind in the mental body.

While the other layers will dissipate in time, this layer will always exist, even after death. After death, it will reincarnate in newly formed physical bodies with the information accumulated in previous lives, enabling this layer to be accessed for the Akashic[4] records by a few individuals who have the ability to do so.

This layer is described as an extremely bright golden light that is rapidly pulsating. This golden light is composed of tiny golden silver threads spreading throughout the layer.

---

[4]Believed to have all of a person's information about past lives. Edgar Cayce used to access this in his readings of clients.

Etheric Template Layer

(Fig. 7) Etheric Template Layer

Celestial Layer

(Fig.8) Celestial Layer

Ketheric Layer

(Fig.9) Ketheric Layer

In learning and straightway practicing,
is there not pleasure also?

-Confucius

Seeing Auras

four

The majority of people cannot see the Aura, although experienced Reiki Healers can sense and feel its presence. There is a select group of people who can see the Aura naturally and that group is usually made up of Psychics and Medical Intuitives. The ability of this group who can see Auras ranges from seeing just a hazy mist around the body to seeing the actual colors. The list gets shorter for the people who can see the colors beyond the first three layers, and most of the time they will actually just sense or have a knowing of these colors.

There are a few people in the above group who are not only able to see the colors, but can also read (interpret) them for illness and disease. Reading Aura colors for illness and disease is very subjective and should be left to experienced readers.

Maybe you can see Aura colors now, or will discover that you are able to see Aura colors with the methods in this chapter. Either way, I believe that in order to give effective and correct readings of a person's Aura, you have to develop your own interpretations of the colors.

There are many charts and books available that give you the author's meanings of the Aura colors. They are a good place to get a basic foundation for comparison with your own interpretations. I have included a list of the common readings of the basic colors in the back of this book for your review; but remember, it is only a guide.

The challenge with going strictly by charts and books in reading Aura colors is that not all people perceive colors the same way. Color is determined in your brain via your eyes. What I might perceive as purple you might perceive as light red, for example. Another difficulty is each person's Aura is individual and unique and so are their color combinations. A color described as "normal" for people in general in one book or chart, could be an "abnormal" color for a few individuals.

If you give out incorrect information in an Aura Reading, even once, it can be harmful to the person receiving it. I am not discouraging you from the pursuit of reading Auras if you are among the select few with this ability, just know that it may take years of practice and experience to get it right.

Reading Aura Colors

If you can see Aura colors and would like to learn to read them, start observing your Reiki clients as you perform Reiki Aura Attunements or during any Reiki session. You know why they are there, so look at the colors in their Aura and make notes of colors matching symptoms and illness and in what state they are mentally and emotionally -- sad, happy, depressed, in love, etc. Observe the colors in their mental and emotion layers during these states. By doing this, over a period of time you will develop your own accurate readings of Auras.

The good news is that it isn't necessary to see Auras or their colors to perform a successful Reiki Aura Attunement.

Seeing Auras

Students always like to try to see Auras. With that in mind, I will explain several methods I like to use.

There are many theories about and methods for seeing the Aura and some are easier than others, but most will work with practice. The two I describe are the simplest and easiest to do. One method is to see the Aura around others, and another is to see the Aura around yourself. Before I explain the two methods, here are a few points to remember in seeing the Aura:

◆ Do not confuse the Aura with the lights seen by people suffering from migraine headaches, bright spots when the eyes are rubbed or the particles (floaters) that sometimes drift in your vision.

◆ Most people cannot see the Aura at all until they practice a method to do so. With practice, the majority will only be able to see a glow or a haze or a mist around the body; but, you might fall into the select group who can see or sense Aura colors.

◆ Even after practicing the following methods, some people still will not be able to see the Aura, and that is not a problem. If you discover you are such a person, do not worry about it. As I mentioned before, the ability to see the Aura is not required to perform successful Reiki Aura Attunements.

◆ Relax, do not strain your eyes when trying to see the Aura and do not be concerned if you cannot see it the first few times.

◆ At the beginning, you might only be able to see the Aura for a few seconds, but in time, it will appear for longer periods.

◆ Bright colored clothing should not be worn by either the person whose Aura you are trying to see or when trying to see your own Aura. If bright colors are worn, this will make seeing the Aura more of a challenge.

◆ The more you practice the following two methods, the odds of your success with seeing the Aura will increase.

◆ If after three minutes you do not see the Aura, stop the process and try again another day.

Seeing Another Person's Aura

1. Have a person stand in front of a white background or solid, light-colored wall. Try to keep the lighting to a minimum.

2. Stand about eight to ten feet in front of this person. (Fig.10)

3. Take several steps to your right or left so you will not be facing the person directly. From the direction you are now standing, focus on the opposite side of their body. (Fig.11)

4. Let your eyes go a little out of focus or look without focusing, especially around the neck and shoulders on this side.

5. After several minutes you might be able to see some sort of haze or white glow around the person on the opposite side - that's the Aura. (Fig.12)

6. Once you are able to see the Aura on one side of a person, you can stand directly in front of them and see their entire Aura. (Fig.13)

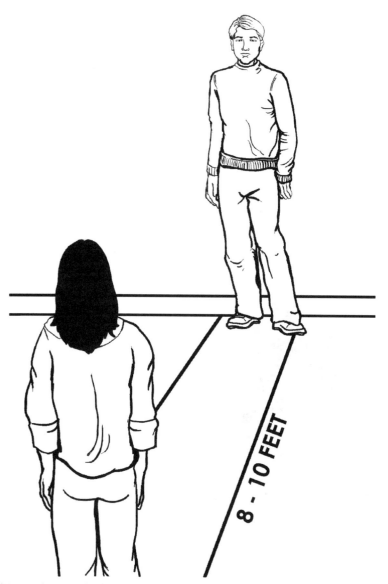

8 - 10 FEET

(Fig.10) Stand about eight to ten feet in front of this person.

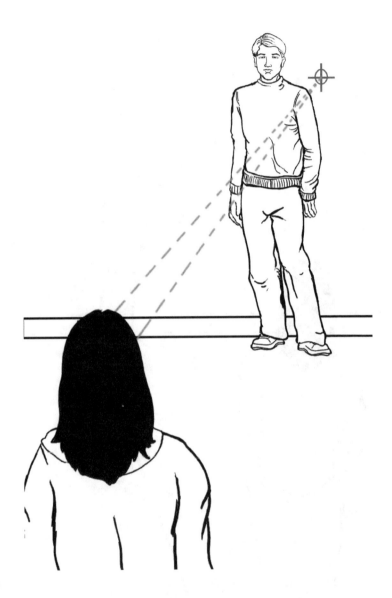

(Fig.11) Take several steps to your right or left so you will not be facing them directly. From the direction you are now standing, focus on the opposite side of their body.

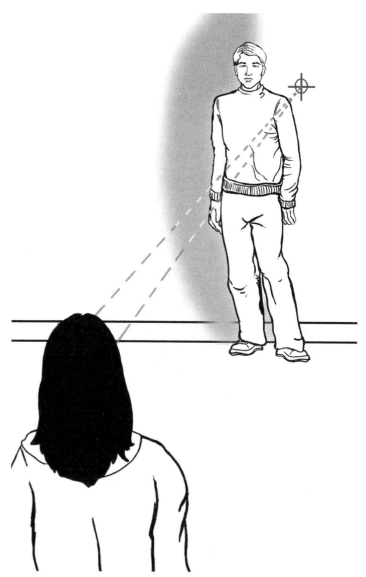

(Fig.12) After several minutes you might be able to see some sort of haze or white glow around the person on the opposite side - that's the Aura.

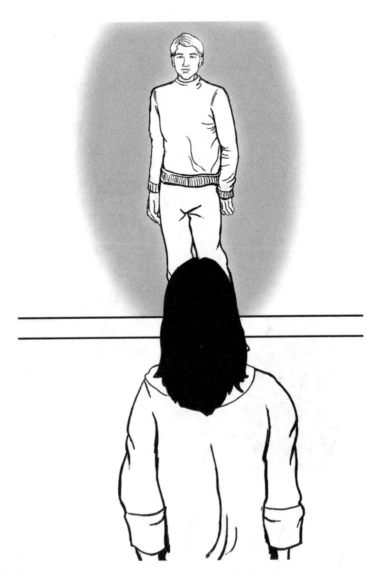

(Fig.13) Once you are able to see the Aura on one side of a person, you can stand directly in front of them and see their entire Aura.

Seeing Your Own Aura

1. Sit about three feet in front of a mirror.

2. Place a lamp with a low wattage bulb and a white shade on a table to your left or right. Make sure the light does not reflect in the mirror or is too bright for your eyes. (Fig.14)

3. Begin by looking at yourself full view, then select one side of your body and focus on it. Look over the reflection of the shoulder of the side you selected. In other words, it's like looking over your own shoulder. (Fig.15)

4. Relax your vision and let your eyes go out of focus.

5. After a few minutes you should begin to see a white glow, haze, or outline, or even colors around the opposite area on which you are focusing. (Fig.16)

6. Once you become accomplished at seeing the Aura on one side of your body, you can then follow the same process to see your full body Aura. Just look at yourself full view, then look over the top of the reflection of your head.

(Fig.14) Place a lamp with a low wattage bulb and a white shade on a table to your left or right. Make sure the light does not reflect in the mirror or is too bright for your eyes.

(Fig.15) Begin by looking at yourself full view, then select one side of your body and focus on it. Look over the reflection of the shoulder of the side you selected. In other words, it's like looking over your own shoulder.

(Fig.16) After a few minutes you should begin to see a white glow, haze, or outline, or even colors around the opposite area on which you are focusing.

Our greatest glory is not in never falling, but in rising every time we fall.

-Confucius

Wherever you go, go with all your heart.
-Confucius

Sensing Auras

five

As I explained in the last chapter, it is a challenge for most people to see Auras without practice, but the majority of people have felt or sensed their presence in themselves and others at one time or another. Through Auras we feel and sense feelings, emotions, thoughts, memories, and other non-physical experiences, even though you may not have connected this to your Aura when this was occurring.

Auras Interact

The Aura is very sensitive and we pick up feelings, emotions, and sometimes thoughts when we come within range of another person's Aura. There are many expressions to describe this, (i.e., "...the person gives me the creeps," "I feel good or bad vibes," "I feel funny about the person," "...the person's energy is good/bad," "...the person doesn't feel right," "...you're in my space," and so on.)

How many times have you met a person and instantly felt uncomfortable around them? Or the opposite, you met a person and felt immediately at ease in their presence? Maybe you came in contact with a person and instantly knew what state they were in emotionally (sad, happy, in love, etc.) or their attitude (good or bad). This information is coming from Auras interacting.

Auras can also attract situations and circumstances. A negative example would be if a person has a fear issue within the emotional layer, they will often be drawn to circumstances which reaffirm this fear. A positive example of this is if a person has a strong love regarding an issue, they can be drawn to circumstances and situations which reaffirm this love.

Aura Protection

Have you ever noticed yourself feeling tired or drained around some people? A person's Aura that is extremely out of balance and not healthy can drain your energy, or attempt to do so. The best protection for your Aura is to keep it balanced, healthy, and free of Psychic Debris (which is described in the next chapter). In this state it will naturally protect itself from energy drain from other Auras. Reiki Aura Attunements will help keep and get the Aura into this state.

I understand that your Aura might not be healthy on all occasions or that it is a "work in progress," so you may need to protect your Aura at various times when you feel it is necessary. Protecting the Aura is not a natural occurrence. Ideally, Auras are healthy and interact and exchange information with other healthy Auras to help you with your life experience. You are not meant to walk around shielded from other Auras, but, unfortunately, the reality is we need to do so on various occasions to protect ourselves. Until you get your Aura healthy, there are several methods to protect the Aura when needed. These methods range from imagining different colors around the Aura to carrying or wearing different protective stones. They will all work. I prefer the following method when it is necessary to protect your Aura.

Protecting Your Aura

Visualize a protective shield or force field (like in Star Trek or Star Wars) around your entire Aura, including your seventh layer. Or, if you have difficulty with visualizing, just use your intent and know or sense that it is there. With this shield or force field in place, nothing can get in or out. What you can do is decide on a word (or words) that will instantly have it manifest in place and a word (or words) that will remove it.

Keep this shield up until you are able to remove yourself from the person or persons from whom you need protection. I advise you to use all Aura protection methods sparingly and once your Aura is healthy and balanced again, there will not be a need for protection.

Reiki
Aura Attunement

Healing Wheel

Learning without thought is labor lost; thought without learning is perilous.

-Confucius

Aura Attunement

SIX

Reiki Aura Attunements are only performed for specific mental and emotional issues and there is a separate and unique Aura Attunement for each issue. This is unlike Reiki Healing Attunements, which are only for physical ailments and diseases and have a formula[5] to determine how to perform the Attunement, depending on the physical ailment or disease.

---

[5]The basis for Reiki The Ultimate Guide Vol. 2.

First Four Layers

When performing Aura Attunements, you will work with the first four layers of the Aura because that's where the mental and emotional layers are.

The location in the Aura you work with during the Aura Attunement is called the Aura Target Area (ATA). This area is very important and in the next few chapters you will learn more about it.

As an interesting side note, if you look up definitions for mental and emotional issues, they either overlap, or, as is the case in some dictionaries, the definitions seem to be one and the same. This is not surprising since the two Aura layers, mental and emotional, are so close together and are interacting moment by moment.

Why Aura Attunements work

Reiki Aura Attunements are successful because you focus and use your intent while channeling Reiki during the Attunement to break up and/or dissolve blockages for specific mental or emotional issues. These blockages in the Aura, what I call "psychic debris," are in your mental and emotional layers. Psychic Debris is called by different names by other Healers and a few examples are "negative thought forms" and "emotional or mental blocks." Whatever it's called, all Healers are aware of it and agree that this phenomenon exists.

I believe that Psychic Debris in these layers, (i.e., negative emotions and mental thoughts that have accumulated over a period of time, sometimes years) results from an individual not processing or releasing the "debris." These accumulated emotions can be fear, grief, anger, hate, etc. The thoughts can be, *I am not successful, I am not worthy, I am a failure*, etc.

As soon as we feel or think about something, it will take residence in the appropriate Aura layer. Normally, if processed, acted upon, and released in a timely manner, these emotions and/or thoughts will not be negative, but instead are just part of the human experience. However, when they are not processed or released, but instead are held onto and embraced by the conscious or unconscious mind, they accumulate in the mental and emotional layers and become Psychic Debris. This is when problems start to manifest.

A high percentage of the root causes of physical illness and ailments start in the mental and emotional layer, then resonate down to the physical body until we consciously become aware of physical symptoms. Of course, you can perform Reiki Healing Attunements once the symptoms manifest in the physical body, but by that time, they could present a serious challenge. It would be best to perform Reiki Aura Attunements before it gets that far. So, the goal of Reiki Aura Attunements is to produce harmony and balance in your complete being, the Aura and physical body by dissolving or eliminating Psychic Debris.

**It does not matter how slowly you go,
so long as you do not stop.**

-Confucius

Reiki Signs

seven

Students and clients always like to know what they should experience during a Reiki Aura Attunement and if there will be any signs to affirm that Reiki is flowing during the Attunement. It is human nature to want to be conscious of signs to confirm something is actually happening during an Attunement.

The majority of the time there are indeed obvious signs and indications during a Reiki Aura Attunement experienced by the person receiving it and/or giving it. But, occasionally there are either minimal signs or no signs experienced during the Attunement. Please do not worry or be concerned about this when and if this happens. It does not mean the Aura Attunement has not been received or will not be successful. When there are minimal signs, or none of which you are consciously aware during an Aura Attunement, the same results will manifest as an Attunement with perceptible signs. With that in mind, I will describe signs that can manifest during an Aura Attunement.

Reiki Is Subtle and Powerful

As I have mentioned in my previous books, Reiki is very powerful, as your life force should be, but Reiki is very subtle when it flows into the Aura and throughout the physical body so that it can be absorbed and used.

If Reiki were like a charge of electricity, there would be major problems with your body accepting and utilizing it. Each succeeding layer of Aura does step down the intensity of the Reiki as it flows into the physical body. Experienced Healers can experience and sense the flow of Reiki with every Attunement they perform. With practice, all new Healers eventually will feel and sense Reiki flowing.

Signs During the Attunement

During an Aura Attunement the signs (experiences) are unique and different each time for the person receiving it and even with the Healer performing it. The reason for this is simple: A person's condition -- physical, mental, emotional -- is constantly changing and evolving for the better or the worse. Plus, every person's circumstances are different when an Attunement is needed and received. All of these variables make each and every Attunement experience unique.

When a person is receiving a Reiki Aura Attunement and even while the Healer is performing the Attunement, mental and emotional signs will manifest more often than with other Reiki Attunements. The reason is that you are performing specific Attunements for mental and emotional issues, hence more mental and emotional signs.

I recommend mentioning to the person receiving an Aura Attunement that during the Attunement there could be signs, and describe a few possibilities to prevent potential fear or surprise. Below are just a few examples of the signs that can be experienced during an Aura Attunement.

◆ Tingling sensations, warmth or cold around the body
◆ Heat from the direction where the Aura Attunement is being performed
◆ Flashes and/or pulsating around the physical body in the auric field

◆ Mental thoughts and memories rushing up to the conscious mind about the issues for which the Attunement is being performed
◆ Physical body feeling lighter
◆ Feelings of unconditional love
◆ Flashes of insight and knowing about the issue for which the Attunement is being performed
◆ Departed loved ones and guides might appear
◆ Relaxed feeling or tingly, vibrating sensations in the Aura or the physical body
◆ Spiritual visions
◆ Out-of-body experiences
◆ Realistic manifestations, such as colors visualized or sensed, music heard, and/or different aromas smelled
◆ Crying, nose running, and various fluids released from the physical body

The signs experienced may be one or a combination of the above, or the person may experience their own unique signs.

As I mentioned before, Reiki signs during an Attunement do not always occur, but if they do, they are a harmless part of the healing process and should not be feared. If it happens to you or a client, just embrace the experience, or at least understand and accept it as part of a cleansing, releasing process that you must go through for healing. It is always temporary.

Reiki Signs for the Healer

At times you may not feel anything if you are performing the Aura Attunement, but the person receiving it will, or vice versa. Usually, both the Healer and the receiver of the Attunement will experience their own Reiki signs. The most common signs the Healer experiences while performing the Aura Attunement are warm to very hot hands, tingling sensations in hands or throughout the body, hands cold to ice cold, possibly even numbness in the hands and/or arms.

After the Attunement

After receiving an Aura Attunement, your whole body may feel lighter and time can feel like it is moving differently for a while. The whole Attunement may even seem like a dream.

Since everyone progresses in an individual manner in terms of healing because of individual circumstances, you might not consciously sense or physically feel anything at first, but change will be taking place unconsciously. Eventually you will start to sense and feel the change in the issue for which you received the Aura Attunement. It might be subtle at first, but as time goes on, you will have more conscious awareness of a change in the issue and you may need to receive additional Aura Attunements for other issues.

Speak the truth, do not yield to anger;
give, if thou art asked for little; by these
three steps thou wilt go near the gods.

-Confucius

Steps Before and After

eight

There are certain steps to follow before and after a Reiki Aura Attunement. In this chapter, I will describe those steps. If you wish to develop your own method for performing these steps and it will accomplish the same goal, feel free to do so.

Preparation for Performing the Attunement

◆ Decide on the Aura Attunement to be performed
◆ Wash hands
◆ Grounding and Clearing
◆ Protection

The Attunement and Specific Issue

Before performing the Aura Attunement you need to know what the mental or emotional issue is, so that you can use the appropriate Aura Attunement. If you are performing the Aura Attunement on yourself, you certainly will know the purpose of the Attunement, but if the Aura Attunement is for another person, you need to find out in advance why it is needed. Once you know the specific Attunement, always review the directions for that Aura Attunement beforehand to make sure you know how to perform it correctly.

Wash Hands

This is a simple step, but an important one. Wash your hands before any Aura Attunement, even if you are going to perform it on yourself. The easiest way is to buy disposable cleaning packets and use them when needed.

Grounding and Clearing

The Healer should always clear and ground him/herself before performing an Aura Attunement. This ensures Reiki will flow through strongly and uninterrupted to and through the Aura and into the body. Experienced Healers usually have their own method and process for doing this before any Reiki session or Attunement and that will work.

One simple and effective way for all levels to do this is by taking a moment to bring Reiki Energy through the top of the head (7th Chakra) all the way down through your body, then out both legs into the earth. Wait a few seconds, then bring it back from the earth, all the way back up both legs and out the top of the head. This whole process should only take a few minutes and usually you will sense a feeling of balance after the process is complete. Again, you can do your own method, as long as it clears and grounds you before performing the Aura Attunement.

Protection

Protecting yourself is very important in all Attunements, but more so with Aura Attunements. "Psychic Debris" can be released during any Reiki Attunement. You want Psychic Debris to be released and/or dissolved during an Aura Attunement, but you just need to protect yourself from it. The amount released during the Attunement can vary depending on the individual and his or her condition and circumstances.

When released during an Attunement, Psychic Debris can attach itself to you and/or linger in the room, waiting to attach itself to somebody else or change future circumstances in a negative way. When Psychic Debris attaches to you or another person, negative emotional charges can be experienced as long as it stays attached and is not destroyed. This is why new Healers who do not protect themselves during a healing session sometimes feel drained, sick, and/or experience strange emotions to which they are unaccustomed. But, as soon as they clear and balance themselves, they are back to normal.

Below are several suggestions for protection. You can also use your own methods.

◆ Visualize or imagine white or golden light filling the area and surrounding you and/or your client.
◆ You can smudge or sage the room, yourself, and/or your clients.
◆ Place Reiki Crystals or Reiki Healing Stones in the corners of the room.
◆ State a prayer asking your higher power, guides, angels, etc., to protect you and/or your client during this time.
◆ Clear the room with Reiki Symbols by drawing and activating them in all corners of the room. (1st Level Healers will not be able to use this suggestion.)

Please make sure you do some or all of the above suggestions, or use your own method(s) for protection. Either way, it can be done rapidly once you are experienced at it.

Send Reiki Ahead

If you are a 2nd Level Reiki Healer or Reiki Master, you can send Reiki to the room or area where the Aura Attunement will take place ahead of time. This can be done when you anticipate working with a difficult mental or emotional issue. Reiki can be sent a few days or any length of time before the Attunement. Just send Reiki (using the Long Distance symbol – Hon Sha Ze Sho Nen) with the intent to start cleansing, clearing, and preparing the area where the Attunement will be performed and it will be there when you arrive.

Steps to Follow After an Aura Attunement

◆ Break the Connection
◆ Clearing Room and Self
◆ Wash Hands and Shower
◆ Sleep and Rest

Break the Connection

After performing the Aura Attunement on another person, rub and/or shake your hands to break the energy connection you formed with them during the Attunement.

Clearing the Room

Even though during the Aura Attunement you had protection, you still want to clear the area and yourself when you have finished. This should only take 30 seconds to do.

Many Healers have their own method for this, which can be used. Here's what I do after the Attunement: I bring more white or golden light into the room, filling it up and at the same time surrounding me. I then ask my source that any and all Psychic Debris remaining, or whatever you wish to call it, be removed and dissolved from the room and myself now.

Wash Hands and Shower

Wash your hands after performing the Aura Attunement and take a shower as soon as possible.

Preparation for Receiving the Attunement

Below are preparation suggestions I recommend you follow before receiving an Aura Attunement. Do as many on the list as you can. The Reiki Aura Attunement will still be received if you cannot follow every suggestion, but follow as many as you can to ensure as effective an Attunement as possible.

- ◆ Limit or stop eating all animal protein 24 hours before the Attunement.
- ◆ Consume only water or juice four to six hours before the Attunement. Limit or stop use of caffeine drinks four to six hours before the Attunement.
- ◆ Stop drinking alcohol 24 hours before the Attunement.
- ◆ Limit sugar 24 hours before the Attunement.
- ◆ Limit or stop smoking four to six hours before the Attunement.

◆ One day before the Attunement, meditate a few minutes upon the reason you need the Reiki Healing Attunement.

Sleep and Rest

After receiving an Aura Attunement, the best thing to do is sleep when there is a chance. This allows your whole being to integrate the Aura Attunement without other distractions.

If I am walking with two other men, each of them will serve as my teacher. I will pick out the good points of the one and imitate them, and the bad points of the other and correct them in myself.

-Confucius

Guidelines and Insight

nine

In the previous chapter you learned the steps to prepare for a Reiki Aura Attunement and what to do after the Attunement. This chapter defines the terminology I use in the directions for performing the Aura Attunements. It also gives guidelines and insight you will need to know to perform the Attunements.

Aura Target Areas

During Aura Attunements I ask you to place the Mental and Emotional Reiki Symbol in seven locations within the Aura (Photo 1). These locations are called "Aura Target Areas" (ATA). The exact ATA in which you will place the symbol and the sequence you will use in placing the symbol will be in the step-by-step directions for Aura Attunements. The ATA used during a specific Attunement is very important because it will be in line with a Chakra's area of influence[6].

Eventually, the Reiki will flow into this Chakra's area of influence after being channeled through the layers of the Aura. This will help if the mental or emotional issue for which the Attunement is performed has started to manifest early stages of physical symptoms in the body.

The sequence used in placing the Reiki Symbol in the ATA during the Aura Attunement is extremely important because it must be the right combination for the specific mental or emotional issue for which the Attunement is being performed.

Placing the Symbol

There are several methods to place the symbols in the ATA and all of them will work. Visualization is one method. Visualization is seeing a picture in your

---

[6]Area in the physical body where a Chakra influences Reiki flow. This concept is fully explained in Reiki The Ultimate Guide Vol. 2.

(Photo 1) Seven locations of the Aura Target Areas

mind's eye. In this case, the picture is a Reiki Symbol. Some Healers have a challenge visualizing, I am one of them. If you have a difficult time visualizing, another way is to just imagine or know a Reiki Symbol is placed in the ATA when you are asked to do so. You can also draw the symbol, then guide it into the ATA. Use the method that is easiest for you.

Activate Symbols

You will be asked to activate Reiki Symbols during the Attunement. When you activate a Reiki Symbol, it generally means you "turn it on," "make it work," "go into action," etc. There are many ways to activate a Reiki Symbol and it depends on the way you were taught or your preference. A few ways to activate a symbol include thinking of its name, saying it out loud if no one is around, or silently if non-attuned Reiki people are present. Or, you can just use your intent to activate the symbol. Activate Reiki Symbols in the way you feel most comfortable.

Visualize and Activate = All in One

At the point in the Aura Attunement Steps when I say "place the symbol in the ATA, then activate it," this should be done almost simultaneously. In fact, when a few Healers visualize a symbol, it's activated automatically and this will work.

Intent: Generic and Root

Intent is your state of mind in knowing Reiki's exact purpose for the Aura Attunement before performing and during the Attunement.

With the Aura Attunement there are two types of intent that can be used during the Attunement, *Generic Intent* and *Root Intent*. The type of intent that you will use depends on the specific Aura Attunement and the information you have before the Attunement with regard to the mental or emotional issue at hand. You will be given guidance with this at the beginning of each Aura Attunement Chapter, but I will now explain the two intents and give examples of each.

Let's start with Generic Intent. For example I am performing a Reiki Aura Attunement for anger, I will state this silently before I begin the Aura Attunement. "This Aura Attunement I am about to perform is for Anger." Then, while I am channeling Reiki during the Attunement, my intent for Reiki is to dissolve and remove all Psychic Debris related to any anger issues.

Now with Root Intent, I know the root cause of the anger, and I use that as my intent. For example, if the person receiving the Attunement knows their anger is linked to their sister and tells you this before the Attunement, you can use that as your intent. Or, if you are giving the Attunement to yourself and you know the anger is linked to your sister, again use that as the intent. So, before you start the Attunement, you state silently the Attunement is for anger related to the sister, and the intent during the Attunement would be to have Reiki dissolve and remove any Psychic Debris related to the anger linked to the sister. Unfortunately, most people usually do not know what the anger's root cause is that has manifested into Psychic Debris, so the intent during the majority of Aura Attunements for anger is Generic. The advantage of using Root Intent, if possible, is that the mental or emotional issues can be cleared up faster and with fewer Attunements.

Focus

Focus is staying in the moment and concentrating on the task at hand. For example, think about nothing else except the intent for a Reiki Aura Attunement when channeling Reiki into the Aura Target Area that is called for in the directions.

It is taught by some Reiki Masters and schools that you can channel Reiki without intent and focus during a Reiki session or Attunement. You do not have to do anything special -- you can let your mind wander and even talk when channeling Reiki because eventually Reiki will go to where it is needed. In performing Aura Attunements, it is completely the opposite. You must have strong intent and focus during the Aura Attunement for it to be effective.

Reiki Symbol Variations

If your Reiki Symbols have variations in the way they are drawn (as shown in the Aura Attunement directions), this is not a problem when using them during the Attunement. You have been attuned to your symbols, so they will be

effective. If you have completely different Reiki Symbols*
you can still use them in Reiki Aura Attunements, but you
need to make sure the symbols you use equate to a Power
Symbol, Long Distance, Mental/Emotional, and Master
Symbol.

Mental and Emotional Symbol

The pivotal Reiki Symbol used in the Aura Attunement
is the Mental and Emotional Symbol. Unlike the Reiki
Healing Attunements for physical ailments and disease[7]
where this symbol is used sparingly, it is an important part
in the Aura Attunements.

Astral Layer

The Aura Target Area and the location where the Reiki
Symbols are placed are found in the Astral Layer. The
reason for this is to make sure the Reiki Symbol's energy
and the Reiki channeled will work within the mental and
emotional layers.

Finding the Astral layer is simple. It's about eight to twelve
inches out from the physical body. The distance I want
you to use during an Aura Attunement is twelve inches
from the body. You can use a ruler for this, but after a few
times, you will know the correct distance just by looking.
A twelve-inch distance is enough to make sure you are
outside the mental and emotional layers and within the
Astral Layer. Do not worry about being completely within

---

*Reiki Symbols are illustrated in the back of this book.
[7]Reiki Healing Attunements presented in Reiki The Ultimate Guide Vol. 2.

the Astral Layer because it can be a few inches different for every person and you might be overlapping into the fifth layer. Your intent during the Attunement will make sure you are working in the right layer.

Position for the Aura Attunement

If you are performing an Aura Attunement on another person, you can do it with the person either lying down (Photo 2) or sitting on a stool or chair, and from either the front (Photo 3) or the back (Photo 4). I prefer to perform the Attunement from the back with the person sitting on a stool. In my directions in the following chapters, I demonstrate performing the Attunement this way, but how you do it is up to you. If you are performing the Attunement on yourself, you have to do it from the front and the easiest way is lying down (Photo 5), but it can be done from a seated position.

Length of an Aura Attunement

Once you become skilled with performing Reiki Aura Attunements, it should never last longer than fifteen to thirty minutes. Of course, there are always exceptions to this and you will know intuitively when an Aura Attunement needs to be longer.

(Photo 2) If you are performing an Aura Attunement on another person, you can do it with the person either lying down (as shown) or sitting on a stool or chair.

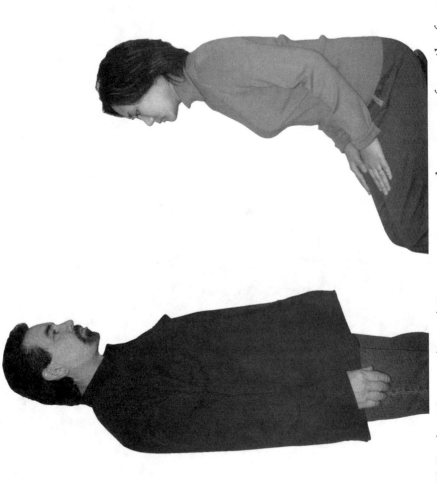

(Photo 3) Performing an Aura Attunement on another person from the front.

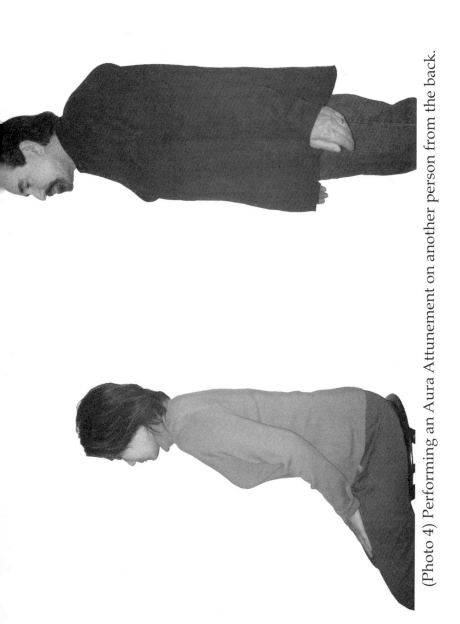

(Photo 4) Performing an Aura Attunement on another person from the back.

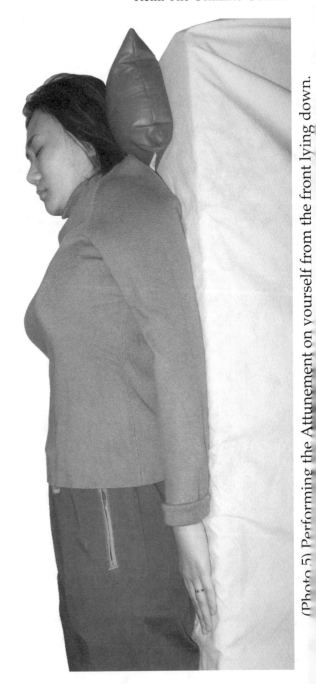

(Photo 5) Performing the Attunement on yourself from the front lying down.

Frequency of Aura Attunements

Perform only one specific Aura Attunement in a single session, then wait a minimum of three days before performing another. Since every person has different circumstances, the amount of Aura Attunements needed for an issue will vary from person to person.

If you or another person has multiple mental or emotional issues that need Attunements, perform the Aura Attunement for the most pressing issue first. You can alternate the Aura Attunements every three days for the other issues.

Study the past, if you would divine the future.

-Confucius

Step By Step

ten

In this chapter, you are going to learn step-by-step how to perform Reiki Aura Attunements on yoursel and others. As an example, I will use the Reiki Aura Attunement for fear (Chapter 17). I will describe performing the Attunement on *yourself or on another person*. With each step I will give an explanation and/or directions. I recommend you read this chapter several times and practice these steps before you perform your first Aura Attunement.

Reiki Aura Attunement for Fear

1. You have prepared for the Aura Attunement.

◆ This is described in Chapter Nine and should be done before every Aura Attunement.

2. You are in the position to either perform the Attunement on yourself (Photo 6) or another person (Photo 7). You are in a quiet area where you will not be disturbed.

◆ As I mentioned in Chapter Nine, there are several positions from which to perform the Attunement on yourself and others. The demonstration photos will show your position from the back when performing on another person and lying down for performing on yourself.

3. State the intent (Generic or Root) for the Aura Attunement silently to yourself before you begin. At this time, you can also ask for guidance during the Attunement. This step should only take a few seconds.

◆ You must make your intent clear regarding which Attunement you are going to perform before you start. For example, with an Aura Attunement for fear you would state, "This Aura Attunement I am about to perform is to dissolve and remove

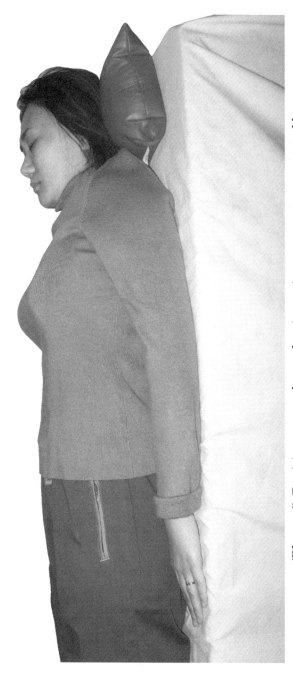

(Photo 6) Position to perform the Aura Attunement on yourself.

(Photo 7) Position to perform the Aura Attunement on another person.

any Psychic Debris for fear issues" if you are using Generic Intent. If you are using Root Intent, then you might say "This Aura Attunement I am about to perform is to dissolve and remove any Psychic Debris regarding [insert receiver's name] fear of rejection." Do this silently and it should only take a few seconds. You can use your own wording as long as the intent is clear.

◆ You can also ask your higher power, source, guardian angel(s), Reiki Guide(s), etc., for guidance during the Aura Attunement at this time.

4. If you are a Reiki Master, place the Master Symbol into the palms of your hands, then activate it (Photo 8). If you are a 1st Level or 2nd Level Healer, omit this step.

◆ Place the Master Symbol into the palms of both of your hands by drawing, visualizing, or knowing it is there. Some Reiki Healers have their own method of placing Reiki Symbols into the palms of their hands before channeling Reiki and that's okay to use. Activate the Master Symbol as described in Chapter Nine. This increases Reiki during the Attunement.

5. If you are a 2nd Level Healer or a Reiki Master, place the Power Symbol into the palms of your hands (Photo 9) and activate it. If you are a 1st Level Healer, omit this step.

(Photo 8) Place the Master Symbol into the palms of your hands, and then activate it.

(Photo 9) Place the Power Symbol into the palms of your hands and activate it.

◆ Place the Power Symbol into the palms of both of your hands by drawing, visualizing, or knowing it is there. As I stated before, some Reiki Healers have their own method of placing Reiki symbols into the palms of their hands before channeling Reiki, and that's okay to use. Activate the symbol as described in Chapter Nine. This increases Reiki during the Attunement.

6. In the next step, place the Mental/Emotional Symbol into the Aura Target Area (Photos 10 and 10b) in the Astral Layer as called for in the Aura directions for the Fear Attunement, then activate the symbol. This *step should only take 15 seconds*. If you are a 1st Level Healer, omit this step.

◆ Place the Mental/Emotion Symbol into the ATA area as described in Chapter Nine. When placing the Reiki Symbol into the ATA, it can be the size of the ATA or smaller. Activate the symbol the way you prefer.

◆ Since I am not a visual person, when I do this step I just simply draw the symbol (Photo 11) in the target area, then I activate it by thinking of its name.

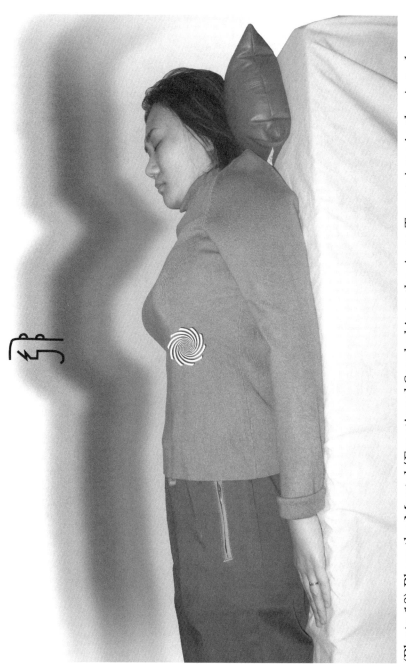

(Photo 10) Place the Mental/Emotional Symbol into the Aura Target Area in the Astral Layer aligned with the third Chakra.

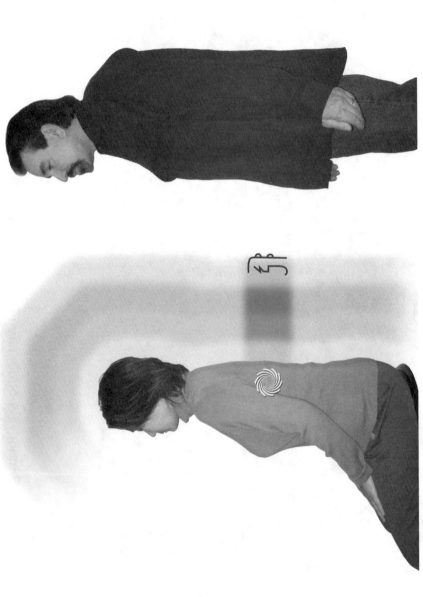

(10b) Place the Mental/Emotional Symbol into the Aura Target Area in the Astral Layer

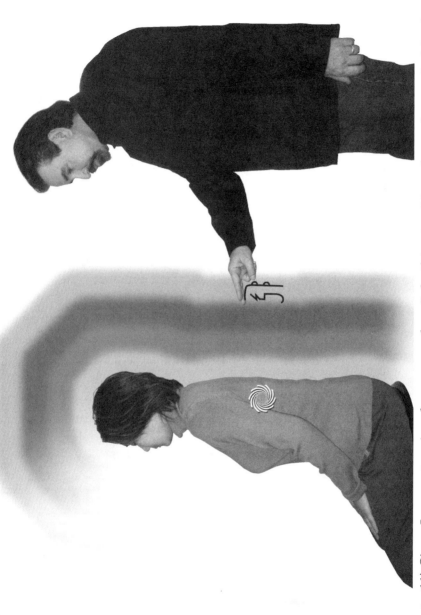

(Photo 11) Since I am not a visual person, when I do this step I just draw the symbol in the target area, then I activate it by thinking of it.

115

7. Now channel Reiki directly into the center of the Aura Target Area (Photos 12 and 12b). Your hand(s) should be about one to two inches away from where you have placed the Mental/Emotional Symbol. Do this with focus and intent (Generic or Root) regarding the purpose of the Aura Attunement (e.g., fear). If you are a 1st Level Healer, you would do the same as above, but of course, you will not have placed the Mental/Emotional Symbol there. This step should only take about two minutes.

◆ This is a very important step. Your hand (or hands) should be directly in front of and aligned with the ATA about one to two inches away. Do the alignment the best you can. Next, channel Reiki into the center of this area. This ensures Reiki will flow through the Astral Layer, through the Mental and Emotional Layers, dissolving and removing Psychic Debris with regard to the purpose for which the Attunement is intended. The Reiki will continue to flow into the physical body and into the Chakra's Area of Influence that is aligned with the ATA in the Aura Attunement directions. This means you will have to move and adjust your hand (or hands) depending on the ATA required in a specific Attunement.

◆ When you are channeling the Reiki, make sure you are focused and your intent (Generic or Root) is for the Reiki to dissolve and remove Psychic Debris for the specific mental or emotional issue for which the Attunement is intended. In this example it is fear.

(Photo 12) Channel Reiki directly into the center of the Aura Target Area. Your hand(s) should be about one to two inches away from where you have placed the Symbol.

117

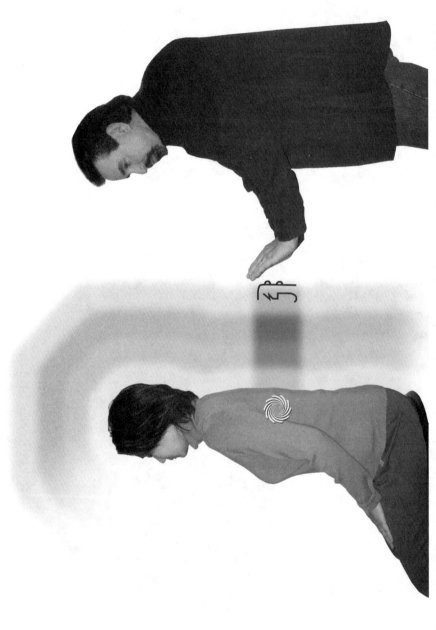

(Photo 12b) Channel Reiki directly into the center of the Aura Target Area. Your hand(s)

◆ The 1st Level Healer performs this step and follows the same directions, except they do not place a Mental/Emotional Symbol into the ATA.

8. The next step is the same as Step Six, but working with a different ATA. Place the Mental/Emotional Symbol into the Aura Target Area (Photos 13 and 13b) in the Astral Layer as called for in the Aura directions for the Fear Attunement, and then activate the symbol. This step should only take 15 seconds. If you are a 1st Level Healer, omit this step.

◆ You will work with two ATAs during an Aura Attunement. The sequence you work with depends on the specific Attunement directions.

◆ Place the Mental/Emotional Symbol into the ATA area as described in Chapter Nine. When placing the Reiki Symbol into the ATA, it can be the size of the ATA or smaller. Activate the symbol the way you prefer.

◆ As I mentioned before, I am not a visual person so when I do this step, I just draw the symbol in the target area, then I activate it by thinking of its name.

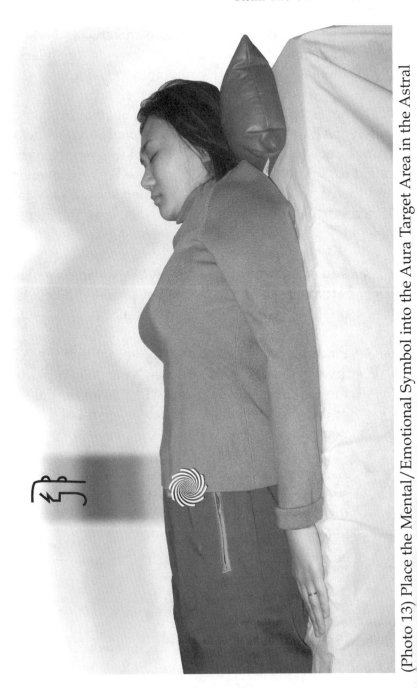

(Photo 13) Place the Mental/Emotional Symbol into the Aura Target Area in the Astral

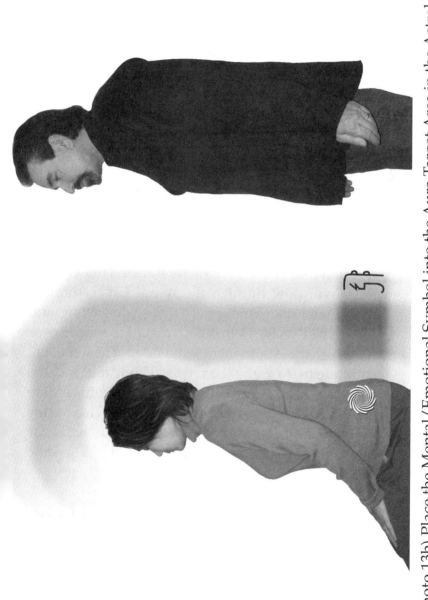

(Photo 13b) Place the Mental/Emotional Symbol into the Aura Target Area in the Astral Layer aligned with the first Chakra.

9. This next step is the same as Step Seven, but working with a different ATA. Channel Reiki directly into the center of the Aura Target Area (Photos 14 and 14b). Your hand(s) should be about one to two inches away from where you have placed the Mental/Emotional Symbol. Do this with focus and intent (Generic or Root) regarding the purpose for which the Aura Attunement is intended (e.g., fear.) If you are a 1st Level Healer, you will do the same, but you have not placed the Mental/Emotional Symbol into the ATA. This step should only take about two minutes.

◆ Again, this is a very important step. Your hand (or hands) should be directly in front of and aligned with the ATA about one to two inches away. Do the alignment the best you can. Next, channel Reiki directly into the center of this area. This ensures Reiki will flow through the Astral Layer, through the Mental and Emotional Layers, dissolving and removing Psychic Debris with regard to the purpose for which the Attunement is intended. The Reiki will continue to flow into the physical body and into the Chakra's Area of Influence that is aligned with the ATA in the Aura Attunement directions. This means you will have to move and adjust your hand (or hands) depending on the ATA required in a specific Attunement.

◆ When you are channeling the Reiki, make sure you are focused and your intent (Generic or Root) is for the Reiki to dissolve and remove Psychic Debris for the specific mental or emotional issue for which the Attunement is intended. In this example it is fear.

(Photo 14) Channel Reiki directly into the center of the Aura Target Area, about one to two inches away from where you have placed the Mental/Emotional Symbol.

(Photo 14b) Channel Reiki directly into the center of the Aura Target Area, about one to

◆ The 1st Level Healer performs this step and follows the same directions, except they do not place a Mental/Emotional Symbol into the ATA.

10. The Attunement is complete.

◆ Perform the finishing steps described in Chapter Eight

At first glance the steps with the explanations might seem like a lot to remember, but once you have performed a few Aura Attunements, the steps will seem like second nature. Let's take a look at the directions for an Aura Attunement for fear without the explanations for the steps and you will see how easily the steps flow.

Reiki Aura Attunement for Fear
[2nd Level Healers and Reiki Masters]

1. You have prepared for the Aura Attunement.

2. You are in the proper position to either perform the Attunement on yourself or another person. You are in a quiet area where you will not be disturbed.

3. State the intent (Generic or Root) for the Aura Attunement silently to yourself before you begin. At this time, you can also ask for guidance during the Attunement. *This step should only take a few seconds.*

4. If you are a Reiki Master, place the Master Symbol into the palms of your hands, then activate it. *2ⁿᵈ Level Healers must omit this step.*

5. Place the Power Symbol into the palms of your hands and activate it.

6. Place the Mental/Emotional Symbol into the Aura Target Area in the Astral Layer as called for in the directions, then activate it. *This step should only take 15 seconds.*

7. Now channel Reiki directly into the center of the Aura Target Area. Your hand(s) should be about one to two inches away from where you have placed the Mental/ Emotional Symbol. Do this with focus and intent (Generic or Root) regarding the purpose of the Aura Attunement (e.g., fear). *This step should only take about two minutes.*

8. In the next step, place the Mental/Emotional Symbol into the second Aura Target Area in the Astral Layer as called for in the directions, then activate the symbol. *This step should only take 15 seconds.*

9. Now channel Reiki directly into the center of the second Aura Target Area. Your hands should be about one to two inches away from where you have placed the Mental/ Emotional Symbol. Do this with focus and intent (Generic or Root) regarding the purpose of the Aura Attunement.

10. The Attunement is complete. Perform the finishing steps described in Chapter Eight.

Reiki Aura Attunement for Fear
[1st Level Healers]

1. You have prepared for the Aura Attunement.

2. You are in the proper position to either perform the Attunement on yourself or another person. You are in a quiet area where you will not be disturbed.

3. State the intent (Generic or Root) for the Aura Attunement silently to yourself before you begin. At this time, you can also ask for guidance during the Attunement. *This step should only take a few seconds.*

4. Now channel Reiki directly into the center of the Aura Target Area as called for in the directions. Your hands should be about one to two inches away from the Astral Layer. Do this with focus and intent (Generic or Root) regarding the purpose of the Aura Attunement (e.g., fear). *This step should only take about two minutes.*

5. Next channel Reiki directly into the center of the second Aura Target Are as called for in the directions. Your hands should be about one to two inches away from the Astral Layer. Do this with focus and intent (Generic or Root) regarding the purpose of the Aura Attunement (e.g., fear). *This step should only take about two minutes.*

6. The Attunement is complete. Perform the finishing steps described in Chapter Eight.

The best men are born wise. Next come those who grow wise by learning: then, learned, narrow minds. Narrow minds, without learning, are the lowest of the people.

-Confucius

Final Review

Here is a review of important points about Reiki Aura Attunements. You should know them thoroughly before performing your first Aura Attunement.

◆ The Reiki Aura Attunements are for mental or emotional issues. Ascertain the issue beforehand and perform the appropriate Attunement.

◆ In every Aura Attunement's set of directions there are two Aura Target Areas and the correct sequence to use them during the Attunement. You need to follow this sequence exactly. If you have any questions about performing any step(s), always refer back to Chapter 10 for a review.

◆ Reiki 1st Level Healers will omit steps *four, five, six,* and *eight* in all the Aura Attunement directions, but will still channel Reiki to the Aura Target Area with the intent needed for each Aura Attunement.

◆ As I previously mentioned, there are several positions from which to perform the Attunement on yourself and others. The Aura Attunement directions will show the Aura Target Areas from two different positions, one lying down and one from behind, the two positions that I recommend using when performing the Attunements. If you desire to perform the Attunements on yourself or another person in a sitting position from the front, just use the photos with the ATAs in the back as a guide, and bring them to the front of the body.

◆ When performing an Aura Attunement on another person and the directions call for an ATA that's in line with the 7th Chakra's Area of Influence, you must move closer to the person and place your hand(s) above the person's head to channel Reiki directly into the center (Photo 14c). If you are performing the Attunement on yourself, simply place your hand(s) above your own head to channel Reiki (Photo 14d).

♦ Perform only one specific Aura Attunement in a single session, then wait a minimum of three days before performing another. Since every person has different circumstances, the amount of Aura Attunements needed for an issue will vary from person to person.

♦ If you or another person has multiple mental or emotional issues that need Attunements, perform the Aura Attunement for the most pressing issue first. You can alternate the Aura Attunements every three days for the other issues.

♦ If you are a Reiki 2nd Level or Master, you can perform the Aura Attunements without using the Reiki Symbols, if you desire. Just follow the Reiki 1st Level steps for the Attunements.

♦ When channeling Reiki during the Aura Attunement, you can use one or two hands.

♦ Make sure you know what type of intent, Generic or Root, you will use during the Attunement. If it is Root, you will need to know precisely what it is before the Attunement is performed for ultimate effectiveness.

131

(Photo 14c) Move closer to the person and place your hand(s) above the person's head to

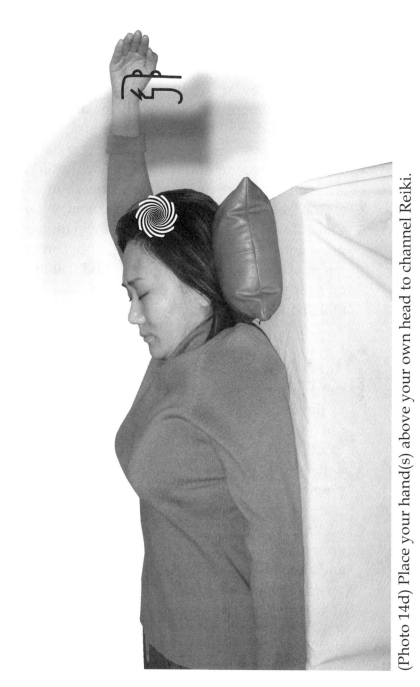

(Photo 14d) Place your hand(s) above your own head to channel Reiki.

◆ When placing the Reiki Symbol into the ATA, it can be the size of the ATA or smaller. Do not be concerned with perfection when doing this. Just do the best you can. If you are a little off in the placement or size of the symbol, your intent will make the needed adjustment during the Attunement.

◆ There are three important items that make an Aura Attunement effective. One, the sequence in which each ATA is used during the Attunement. Two, the Chakra's Area of Influence that the Reiki ultimately flows into when being channeled, and Three, the intent of the Attunement. You will find that in each of the specific Aura Attunements the exact sequence of using the ATAs is never the same.

◆ If you are a 1st Level Healer you can still perform Aura Attunements, but you have to omit certain steps in the directions. Once you become attuned to the Reiki 2nd and Master Level symbols, you can use the Reiki Symbols. You can become attuned to the higher Reiki Levels through your previous Reiki Master or use one my Reiki Attunement DVD programs.

◆ When channeling Reiki during the Aura Attunement, your hand (or hands) should be directly in front of and aligned with the ATA, about one to two inches away from where you placed the symbol. Do the alignment the best you can. You always channel Reiki directly into the center of this area. This ensures Reiki will flow through the Astral Layer, through the Mental and Emotional Layers, dissolving and removing Psychic Debris for which the Attunement is intended. The Reiki will continue to flow into the Chakra's Area of Influence in the physical body that is aligned with the ATA in the Aura Attunement directions. This means you will have to move and adjust your hand (or hands) depending on the ATA required in a specific attunement.

◆ If there are differences in your Aura teachings compared with mine, do not worry. Teachings can be very subjective and usually the differences are minor. All Aura teachings acknowledge a Mental and Emotional layer in the Aura.

◆ Talk only when necessary during the Aura Attunement. Maintain strong intent and focus throughout the entire Attunement.

◆ The power of the Reiki Symbols does not come from drawing, visualizing, or imagining them perfectly, so do not worry about this. The power comes from your intent to activate the symbol(s) once you have been attuned to them. Just activate the Reiki Symbols the best you can during the Aura Attunement.

"In the following chapters are step-by-step instructions regarding the specific Reiki Aura Attunements. In each chapter there are two sets of photos for the ATA: one set shows how to perform the Aura Attunement on yourself and the other set shows how to perform the Aura Attunement on another person."

135

Life is really simple, but we insist on making it complicated.

-Confucius

Specific Reiki
Aura Attunements

Healing Wheel

What you do not want done to yourself, do not do to others.

-Confucius

Reiki Aura Attunement
Addiction

twelve

Intent

Use Root Intent for the specific addiction: smoking, caffeine, sugar, etc. Generic Intent is rarely used and not recommended.

Aura Attunement for Addictions

1. You have prepared for the Aura Attunement.

2. You are in the proper position to either perform the Attunement on yourself or another person in a quiet area where you will not be disturbed.

3. State the intent for the Aura Attunement silently to yourself before you begin. At this time, you can also ask for guidance during the Attunement. *Step should only take a few seconds.*

4. If you are a Reiki Master, place the Master Symbol into the palms of your hands, then activate it. **2nd Level Healers omit this step.**

5. Now place the Power Symbol into the palms of your hands and activate it.

6. Next place the Mental/Emotional Symbol into the Aura Target Area in the Astral Layer that is aligned with the first Chakra as shown (Photos 15 and 15b), then activate the symbol. *Step should only take 15 seconds.*

7. Now channel Reiki directly center into the Aura Target Area from about one to two inches away from where you have placed the Mental/Emotional Symbol. Do this with focus and the intent you have decided upon. *Step should only take about 2 minutes.*

8. Next, place the Mental/Emotional Symbol into the second Aura Target Area in the Astral Layer that is aligned with the fifth Chakra as shown (Photos 16 and 16b), then activate the symbol. *Step should only take 15 seconds.*

9. Now channel Reiki directly center into the Aura Target Area from about one to two inches away from where you have placed the Mental/Emotional Symbol. Do this with focus and the intent you have decided upon. *Step should only take about 2 minutes*

10. The Attunement is complete. Perform the finishing steps.

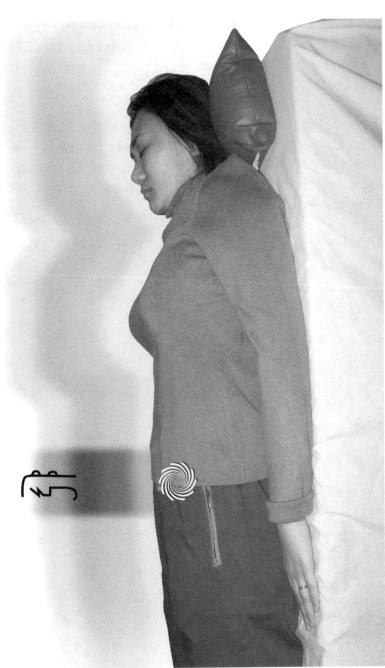

(Photo 15) Place the Mental / Emotional Symbol into the Aura Target Area in the Astral

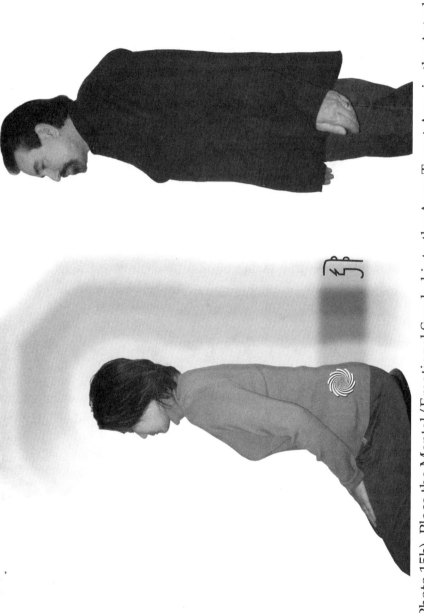

(Photo 15b) Place the Mental/Emotional Symbol into the Aura Target Area in the Astral Layer that is aligned with the first Chakra.

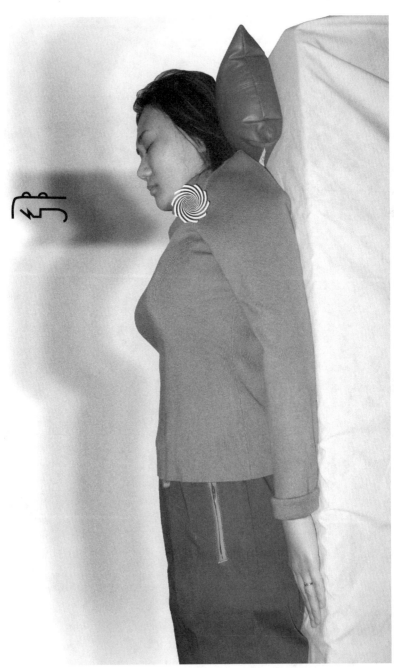

(Photo 16) Place the Mental/Emotional Symbol into the Aura Target Area in the Astral

(Photo 16b) Place the Mental/Emotional Symbol into the Aura Target Area in the Astral Layer that is aligned with the fifth Chakra.

To be fond of learning is near to wisdom.
-Confucius

Reiki Aura Attunement
Anger

Intent

The Root Intent for this Attunement can be anger, specifically for a person, circumstance, place, or thing. If the cause of the anger is not known, use Generic Intent.

1. You have prepared for the Aura Attunement.

2. You are in the proper position to either perform the Attunement on yourself or another person in a quiet area where you will not be disturbed.

3. State the intent for the Aura Attunement silently to yourself before you begin. At this time, you can also ask for guidance during the Attunement. *Step should only take a few seconds.*

4. If you are a Reiki Master, place the Master Symbol into the palms of your hands, then activate it. **2nd Level Healers omit this step.**

5. Now place the Power Symbol into the palms of your hands and activate it.

6. Next place the Mental/Emotional Symbol into the Aura Target Area in the Astral Layer that is aligned with the third Chakra as shown (Photos 17 and 17b), then activate the symbol. *Step should only take 15 seconds.*

7. Now channel Reiki directly into the Aura Target Area about one to two inches away from where you have placed the Mental/Emotional Symbol. Do this with focus and the intent you have decided upon. *Step should only take about 2 minutes.*

8. Next, place the Mental/Emotional Symbol into the second Aura Target Area in the Astral Layer that is aligned with the fourth Chakra as shown (Photos 18 and 18b), then activate the symbol. *Step should only take 15 seconds.*

9. Now channel Reiki directly into the Aura Target Area about one to two inches away from where you have placed the Mental/Emotional Symbol. Do this with focus and the intent you have decided upon. *Step should only take about 2 minutes.*

10. The Attunement is complete. Perform the finishing steps.

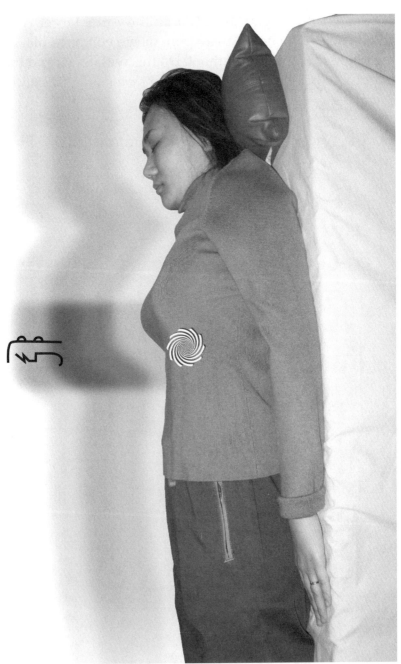

(Photo 17) Place the Mental/Emotional Symbol into the Aura Target Area in the Astral

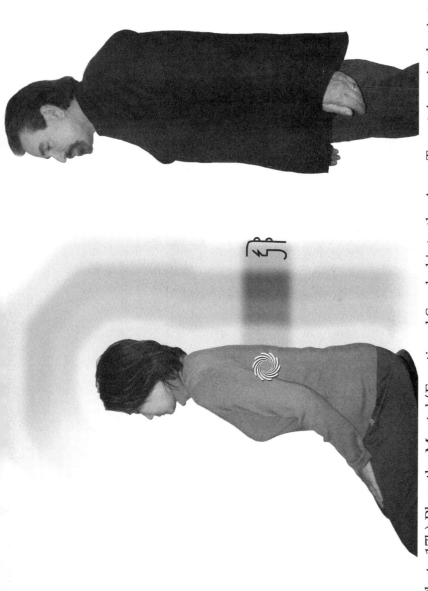

(Photo 17b) Place the Mental/Emotional Symbol into the Aura Target Area in the Astral Layer that is aligned with the third Chakra.

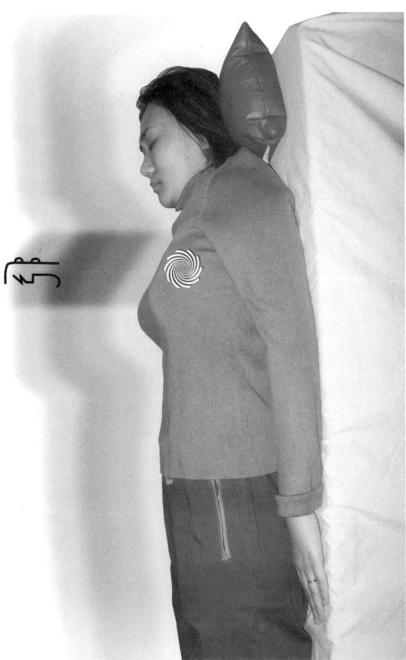

(Photo 18) Place the Mental/Emotional Symbol into the Aura Target Area in the Astral

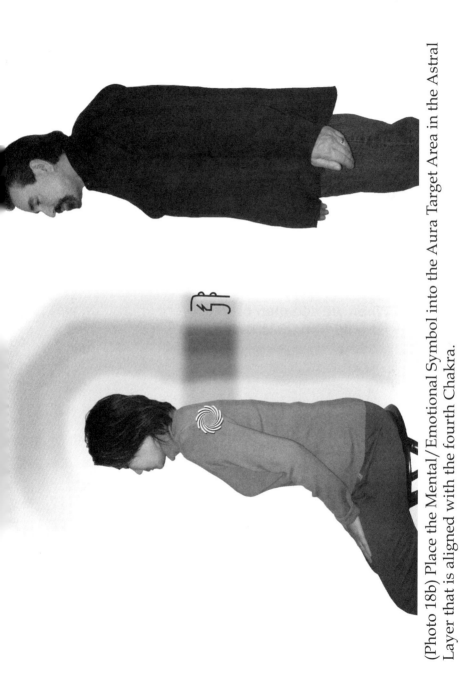

(Photo 18b) Place the Mental/Emotional Symbol into the Aura Target Area in the Astral Layer that is aligned with the fourth Chakra.

When we see men of a contrary character, we should turn inwards and examine ourselves.
-Confucius

Reiki Aura Attunement
Anxiety / Stress

fourteen

Intent

Anxiety and stress are usually linked together. The Root Intent for this Attunement should be the cause for the anxiety or stress. If the cause is not known, use Generic Intent.

1. You have prepared for the Aura Attunement.

2. You are in the proper position to either perform the Attunement on yourself or another person in a quiet area where you will not be disturbed.

3. State the intent for the Aura Attunement silently to yourself before you begin. At this time, you can also ask for guidance during the Attunement. *Step should only take a few seconds.*

4. If you are a Reiki Master, place the Master Symbol into the palms of your hands, then activate it. ***2nd Level Healers omit this step.***

5. Now place the Power Symbol into the palms of your hands and activate it.

6. Next place the Mental/Emotional Symbol into the Aura Target Area in the Astral Layer that is aligned with the third Chakra as shown (Photos 19 and 19b), then activate the symbol. *Step should only take 15 seconds.*

7. Now channel Reiki directly into the Aura Target Area about one to two inches away from where you have placed the Mental/Emotional Symbol. Do this with focus and the intent you have decided upon. *Step should only take about 2 minutes.*

8. Next, place the Mental/Emotional Symbol into the second Aura Target Area in the Astral Layer that is aligned with the fifth Chakra as shown (Photos 20 and 20b), then activate the symbol. *Step should only take 15 seconds.*

9. Now channel Reiki directly into the Aura Target Area about one to two inches away from where you have placed the Mental/Emotional Symbol. Do this with focus and the intent you have decided upon. *Step should only take about 2 minutes.*

10. The Attunement is complete. Perform the finishing steps.

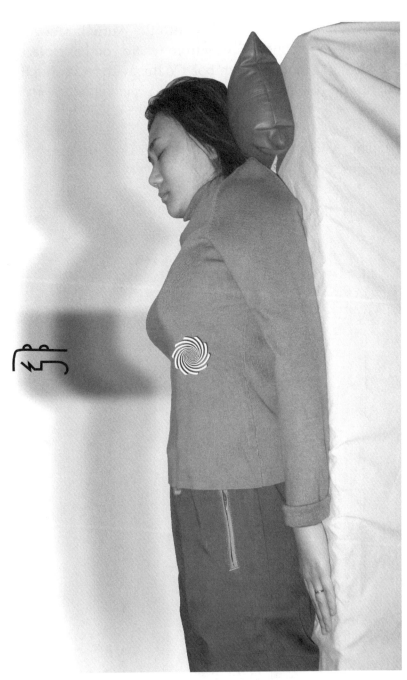

(Photo 19) Place the Mental/Emotional Symbol into the Aura Target Area in the Astral

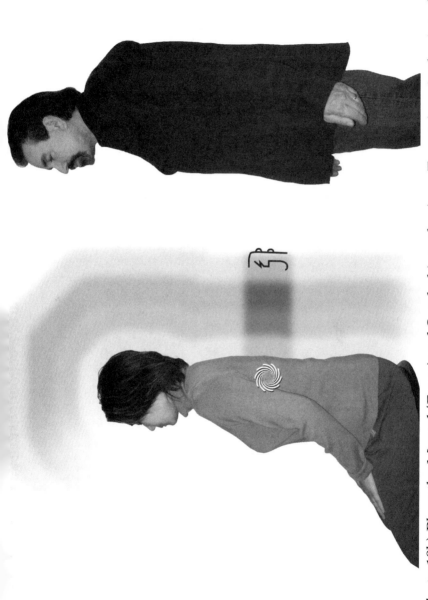

(Photo 19b) Place the Mental/Emotional Symbol into the Aura Target Area in the Astral Layer that is aligned with the third Chakra.

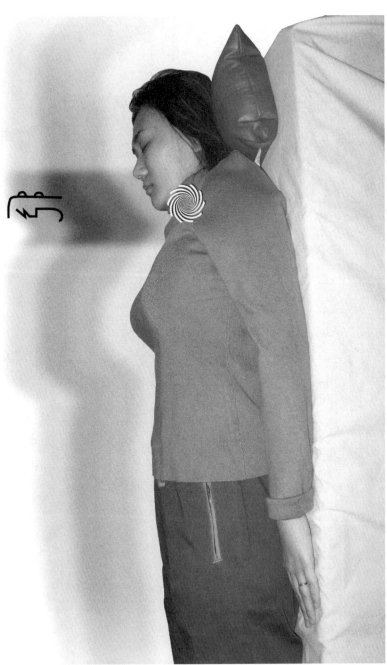

(Photo 20) Place the Mental/Emotional Symbol into the Aura Target Area in the Astral

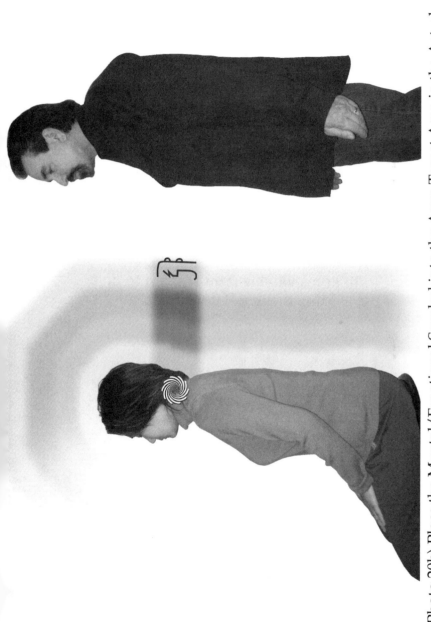

(Photo 20b) Place the Mental/Emotional Symbol into the Aura Target Area in the Astral Layer that is aligned with the fifth Chakra.

161

**To know what is right and not to do it
is the worst cowardice.**

-Confucius

Reiki Aura Attunement
Depression

Intent

The intent used for this Attunement most likely will not be known, so use Generic Intent. Use Root Intent if the source of depression is uncovered.

1. You have prepared for the Aura Attunement.

2. You are in the proper position to either perform the Attunement on yourself or another person in a quiet area where you will not be disturbed.

3. State the intent for the Aura Attunement silently to yourself before you begin. At this time, you can also ask for guidance during the Attunement. *Step should only take a few seconds.*

4. If you are a Reiki Master, place the Master Symbol into the palms of your hands, then activate it. ***2nd Level Healers omit this step.***

5. Now place the Power Symbol into the palms of your hands and activate it.

6. Next place the Mental/Emotional Symbol into the Aura Target Area in the Astral Layer that is aligned with the first Chakra as shown (Photos 21 and 21b), then activate the symbol. *Step should only take 15 seconds.*

7. Now channel Reiki directly into the Aura Target Area about one to two inches away from where you have placed the Mental/Emotional Symbol. Do this with focus and the intent you have decided upon. *Step should only take about 2 minutes.*

8. Next, place the Mental/Emotional Symbol into the second Aura Target Area in the Astral Layer that is aligned with the seventh Chakra as shown (Photos 22 and 22b), then activate the symbol. *Step should only take 15 seconds.*

9. Now channel Reiki directly into the Aura Target Area about one to two inches away from where you have placed the Mental/Emotional Symbol. Do this with focus and the intent you have decided upon. *Step should only take about 2 minutes.*

10. The Attunement is complete. Perform the finishing steps.

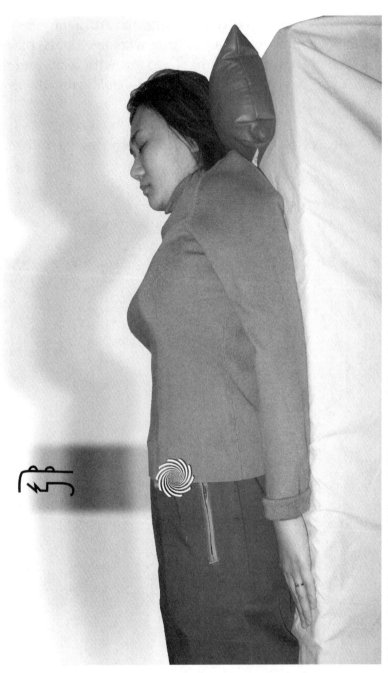

(Photo 21) Place the Mental/Emotional Symbol into the Aura Target Area in the Astral

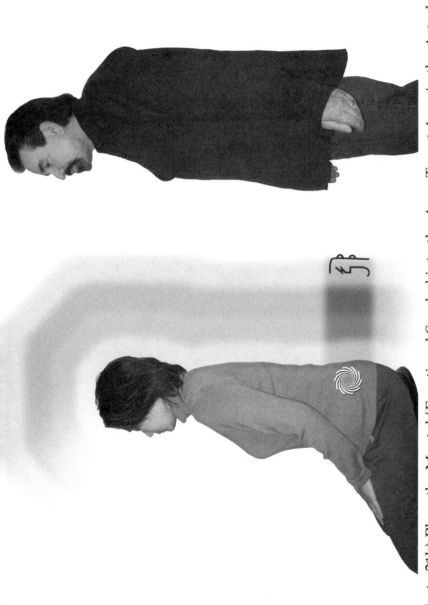

(Photo 21b) Place the Mental/Emotional Symbol into the Aura Target Area in the Astral Layer that is aligned with the first Chakra.

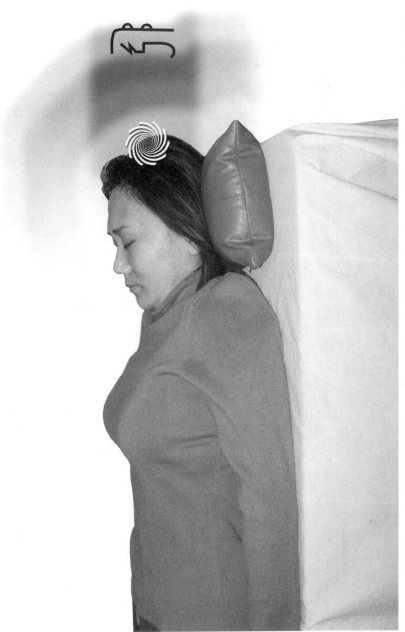

(Photo 22) Place the Mental/Emotional Symbol into the Aura Target Area in the Astral

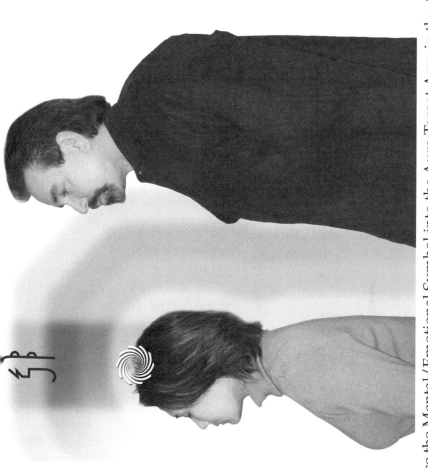

(Photo 22b) Place the Mental/Emotional Symbol into the Aura Target Area in the Astral Layer that is aligned with the seventh Chakra.

**He that would perfect his work
must first sharpen his tools.**

-Confucius

Reiki Aura Attunement
Eating Disorders

Intent

The Intent for this Attunement needs to be for the exact eating disorder that needs to be helped, so Root Intent is always used.

1. You have prepared for the Aura Attunement.

2. You are in the proper position to either perform the Attunement on yourself or another person in a quiet area where you will not be disturbed.

3. State the intent for the Aura Attunement silently to yourself before you begin. At this time, you can also ask for guidance during the Attunement. *Step should only take a few seconds.*

4. If you are a Reiki Master, place the Master Symbol into the palms of your hands, then activate it. **2nd Level Healers omit this step.**

5. Now place the Power Symbol into the palms of your hands and activate it.

6. Next place the Mental/Emotional Symbol into the Aura Target Area in the Astral Layer that is aligned with the first Chakra as shown (Photos 23 and 23b), then activate the symbol. *Step should only take 15 seconds.*

7. Now channel Reiki directly into the Aura Target Area about one to two inches away from where you have placed the Mental/Emotional Symbol. Do this with focus and the intent you have decided upon. *Step should only take about 2 minutes.*

8. Next, place the Mental/Emotional Symbol into the second Aura Target Area in the Astral Layer that is aligned with the fourth Chakra as shown (Photos 24 and 24b), then activate the symbol. *Step should only take 15 seconds.*

172

9. Now channel Reiki directly into the Aura Target Area about one to two inches away from where you have placed the Mental/Emotional Symbol. Do this with focus and the intent you have decided upon. *Step should only take about 2 minutes.*

10. The Attunement is complete. Perform the finishing steps.

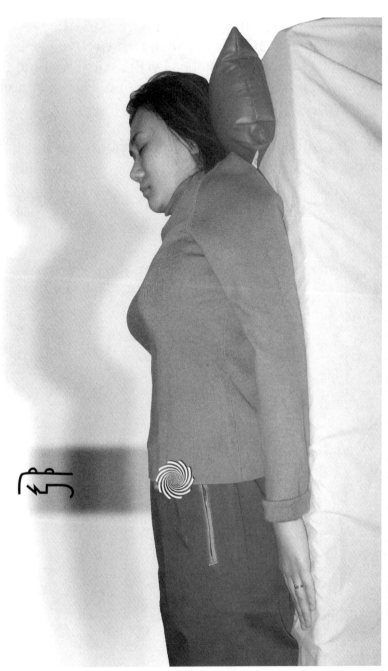

(Photo 23) Place the Mental/Emotional Symbol into the Aura Target Area in the Astral

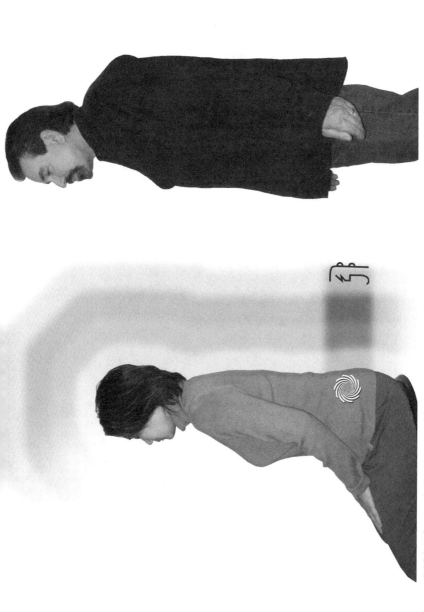

(Photo 23b) Place the Mental/Emotional Symbol into the Aura Target Area in the Astral Layer that is aligned with the first Chakra.

175

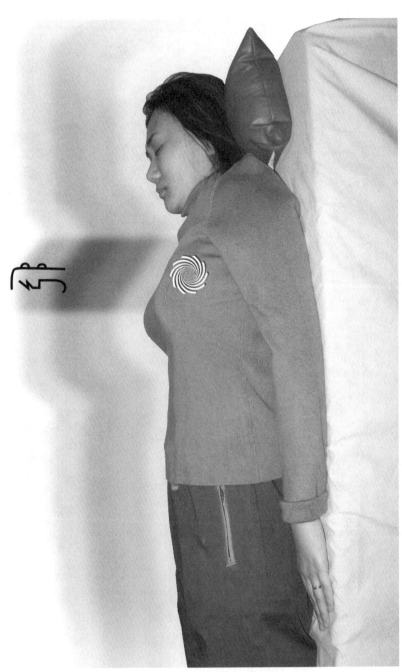

(Photo 24) Place the Mental/Emotional Symbol into the Aura Target Area in the Astral

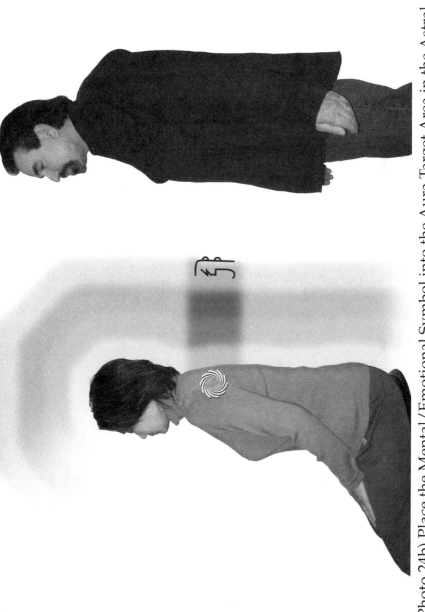

(Photo 24b) Place the Mental/Emotional Symbol into the Aura Target Area in the Astral Layer that is aligned with the fourth Chakra.

The more man meditates upon good thoughts, the better will be his world and the world at large.

-Confucius

Reiki Aura Attunement
Fear

seventeen

Intent

Use Root Intent for this Attunement if the cause of the fear is known, but if not known, use Generic Intent.

1. You have prepared for the Aura Attunement.

2. You are in the proper position to either perform the Attunement on yourself or another person in a quiet area where you will not be disturbed.

3. State the intent for the Aura Attunement silently to yourself before you begin. At this time, you can also ask for guidance during the Attunement. *Step should only take a few seconds.*

4. If you are a Reiki Master, place the Master Symbol into the palms of your hands, then activate it. ***2nd Level Healers omit this step.***

5. Now place the Power Symbol into the palms of your hands and activate it.

6. Next place the Mental/Emotional Symbol into the Aura Target Area in the Astral Layer that is aligned with the third Chakra as shown (Photos 25 and 25b), then activate the symbol. *Step should only take 15 seconds.*

7. Now channel Reiki directly into the Aura Target Area about one to two inches away from where you have placed the Mental/Emotional Symbol. Do this with focus and the intent you have decided upon. *Step should only take about 2 minutes.*

8. Next, place the Mental/Emotional Symbol into the second Aura Target Area in the Astral Layer that is aligned with the first Chakra as shown (Photos 26 and 26b), then activate the symbol. *Step should only take 15 seconds.*

9. Now channel Reiki directly into the Aura Target Area about one to two inches away from where you have placed the Mental/Emotional Symbol. Do this with focus and the intent you have decided upon. *Step should only take about 2 minutes.*

10. The Attunement is complete. Perform the finishing steps.

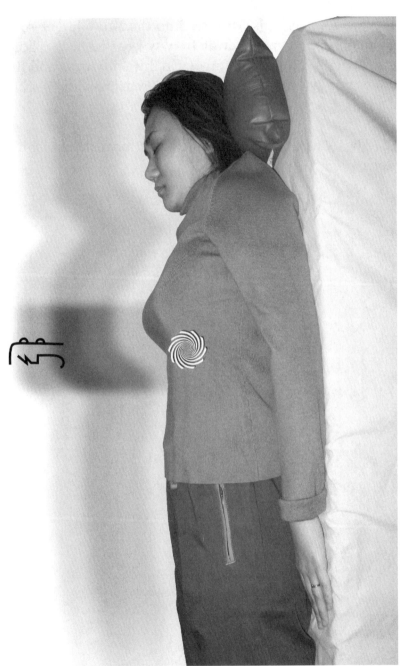

(Photo 25) Place the Mental/Emotional Symbol into the Aura Target Area in the Astral

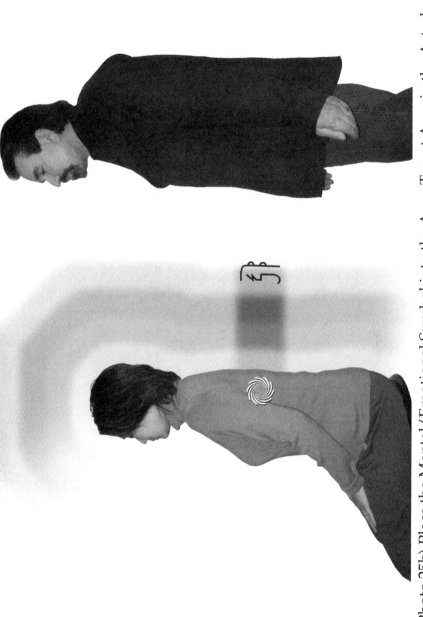

(Photo 25b) Place the Mental/Emotional Symbol into the Aura Target Area in the Astral Layer that is aligned with the third Chakra.

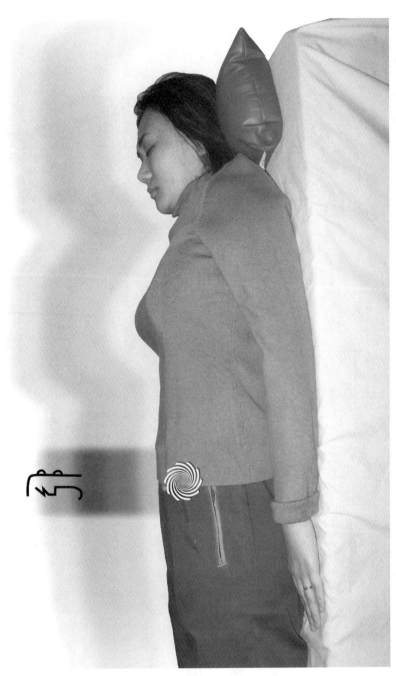

(Photo 26) Place the Mental/Emotional Symbol into the Aura Target Area in the Astral

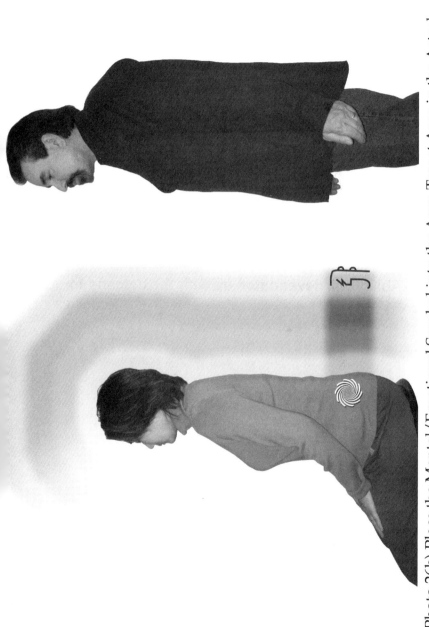

(Photo 26b) Place the Mental/Emotional Symbol into the Aura Target Area in the Astral Layer that is aligned with the first Chakra.

Ability will never catch up with the demand for it.
-Confucius

Reiki Aura Attunement
Grief

Intent

The cause of grief will be usually obvious, so use Root Intent for this Attunement. If the cause is not known, then use Generic Intent.

1. You have prepared for the Aura Attunement.

2. You are in the proper position to either perform the Attunement on yourself or another person in a quiet area where you will not be disturbed.

3. State the intent for the Aura Attunement silently to yourself before you begin. At this time, you can also ask for guidance during the Attunement. *Step should only take a few seconds.*

4. If you are a Reiki Master, place the Master Symbol into the palms of your hands, then activate it. ***2nd Level Healers omit this step.***

5. Now place the Power Symbol into the palms of your hands and activate it.

6. Next place the Mental/Emotional Symbol into the Aura Target Area in the Astral Layer that is aligned with the fourth Chakra as shown (Photos 27 and 27b), then activate the symbol. *Step should only take 15 seconds.*

7. Now channel Reiki directly into the Aura Target Area about one to two inches away from where you have placed the Mental/Emotional Symbol. Do this with focus and the intent you have decided upon. *Step should only take about 2 minutes.*

8. Next, place the Mental/Emotional Symbol into the second Aura Target Area in the Astral Layer that is aligned with the first Chakra as shown (Photos 28 and 28b), then activate the symbol. *Step should only take 15 seconds.*

9. Now channel Reiki directly into the Aura Target Area about one to two inches away from where you have placed the Mental/Emotional Symbol. Do this with focus and the intent you have decided upon. *Step should only take about 2 minutes.*

10. The Attunement is complete. Perform the finishing steps.

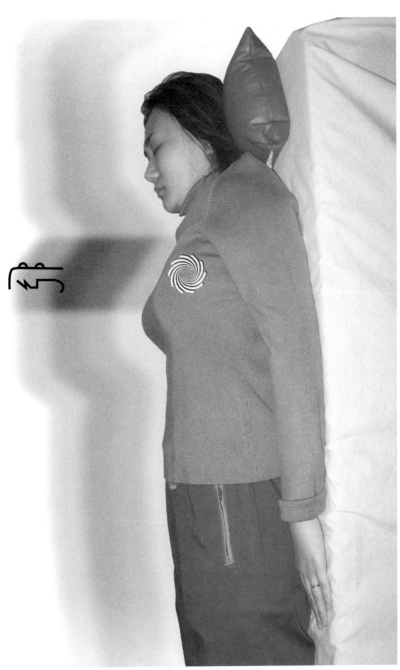

(Photo 27) Place the Mental/Emotional Symbol into the Aura Target Area in the Astral

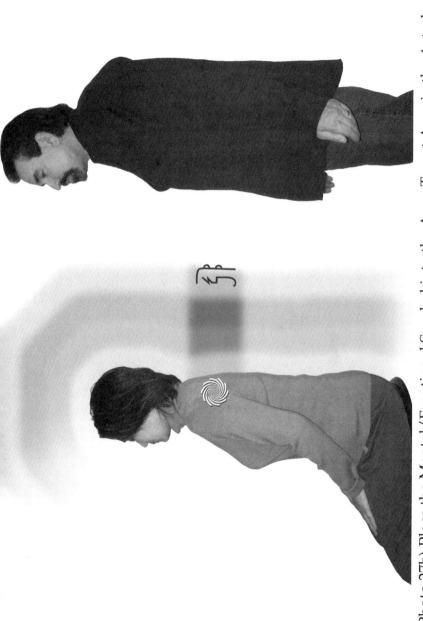

(Photo 27b) Place the Mental/Emotional Symbol into the Aura Target Area in the Astral Layer that is aligned with the fourth Chakra.

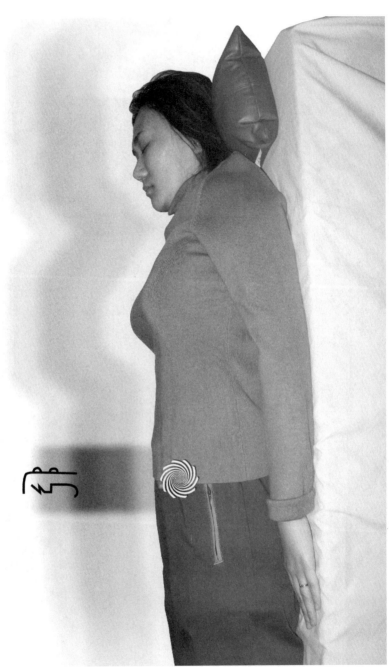

(Photo 28) Place the Mental/Emotional Symbol into the Aura Target Area in the Astral

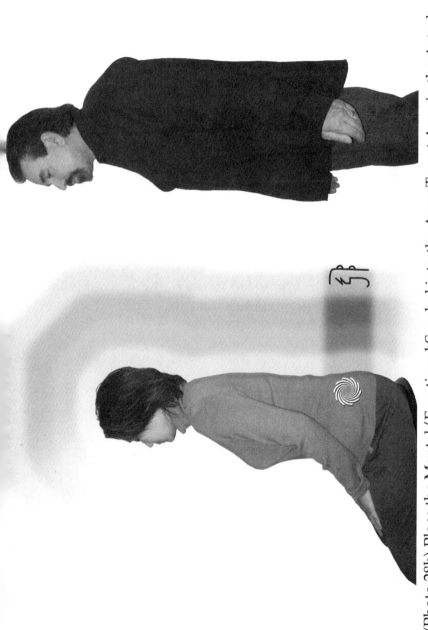

(Photo 28b) Place the Mental/Emotional Symbol into the Aura Target Area in the Astral Layer that is aligned with the first Chakra.

To know is to know you know nothing. That is the true meaning of knowledge.

-Confucius

Reiki Aura Attunement
Guilt

Intent

Use Root Intent for this Attunement if the cause of the guilt is known, but if not known, use Generic Intent.

1. You have prepared for the Aura Attunement.

2. You are in the proper position to either perform the Attunement on yourself or another person in a quiet area where you will not be disturbed.

3. State the intent for the Aura Attunement silently to yourself before you begin. At this time, you can also ask for guidance during the Attunement. *Step should only take a few seconds.*

4. If you are a Reiki Master, place the Master Symbol into the palms of your hands, then activate it. ***2nd Level Healers omit this step.***

5. Now place the Power Symbol into the palms of your hands and activate it.

6. Next place the Mental/Emotional Symbol into the Aura Target Area in the Astral Layer that is aligned with the second Chakra as shown (Photos 29 and 29b), then activate the symbol. *Step should only take 15 seconds.*

7. Now channel Reiki directly into the Aura Target Area about one to two inches away from where you have placed the Mental/Emotional Symbol. Do this with focus and the intent you have decided upon. *Step should only take about 2 minutes.*

8. Next, place the Mental/Emotional Symbol into the second Aura Target Area in the Astral Layer that is aligned with the fourth Chakra as shown (Photos 30 and 30b), then activate the symbol. *Step should only take 15 seconds.*

9. Now channel Reiki directly into the Aura Target Area about one to two inches away from where you have placed the Mental/Emotional Symbol. Do this with focus and the intent you have decided upon. *Step should only take about 2 minutes.*

10. The Attunement is complete. Perform the finishing steps.

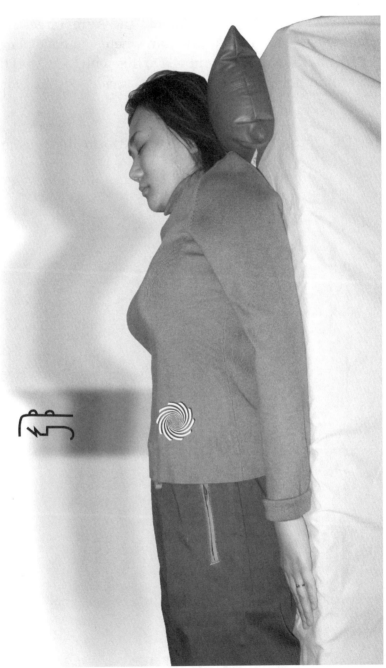

(Photo 29) Place the Mental/Emotional Symbol into the Aura Target Area in the Astral

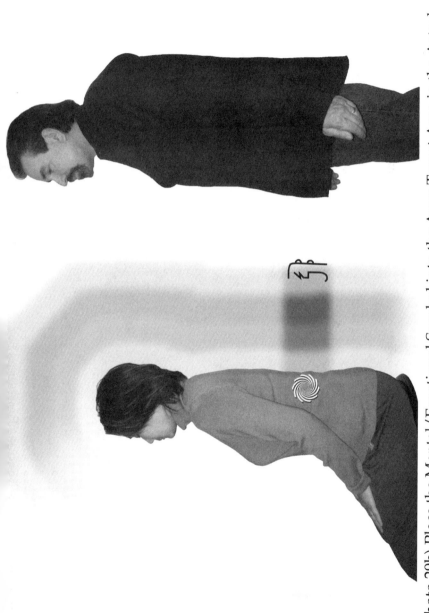

(Photo 29b) Place the Mental/Emotional Symbol into the Aura Target Area in the Astral Layer that is aligned with the second Chakra.

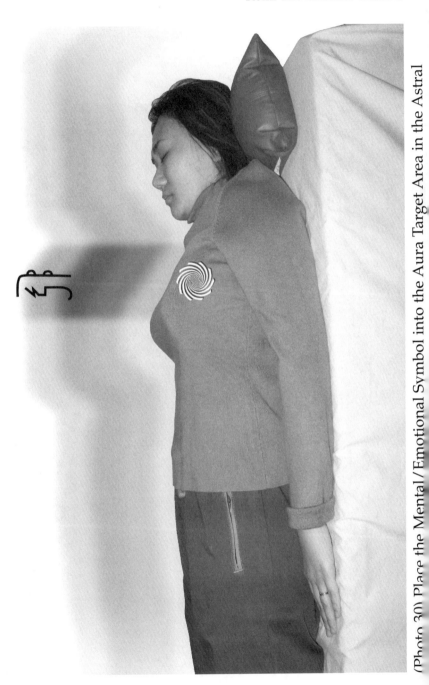

(Photo 30) Place the Mental/Emotional Symbol into the Aura Target Area in the Astral

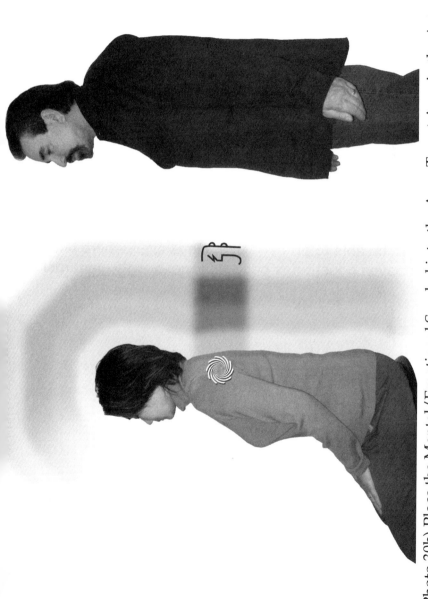

(Photo 30b) Place the Mental/Emotional Symbol into the Aura Target Area in the Astral Layer that is aligned with the fourth Chakra.

To be able to practice five things everywhere under heaven constitutes perfect virtue: gravity, generosity of soul, sincerity, earnestness, and kindness.

-Confucius

Reiki Aura Attunement
Hate

twenty

Intent

Root Intent for this Attunement is usually hatred for a person, place, or thing and is easily found out. Very rarely do you use Generic Intent with this Attunement.

1. You have prepared for the Aura Attunement.

2. You are in the proper position to either perform the Attunement on yourself or another person in a quiet area where you will not be disturbed.

3. State the intent for the Aura Attunement silently to yourself before you begin. At this time, you can also ask for guidance during the Attunement. *Step should only take a few seconds.*

4. If you are a Reiki Master, place the Master Symbol into the palms of your hands, then activate it. **2nd Level Healers omit this step.**

5. Now place the Power Symbol into the palms of your hands and activate it.

6. Next place the Mental/Emotional Symbol into the Aura Target Area in the Astral Layer that is aligned with the fourth Chakra as shown (Photos 31 and 31b), then activate the symbol. *Step should only take 15 seconds.*

7. Now channel Reiki directly into the Aura Target Area about one to two inches away from where you have placed the Mental/Emotional Symbol. Do this with focus and the intent you have decided upon. *Step should only take about 2 minutes.*

8. Next, place the Mental/Emotional Symbol into the second Aura Target Area in the Astral Layer that is aligned with the third Chakra as shown (Photos 32 and 32b), then activate the symbol. *Step should only take 15 seconds.*

9. Now channel Reiki directly into the Aura Target Area about one to two inches away from where you have placed the Mental/Emotional Symbol. Do this with focus and the intent you have decided upon. *Step should only take about 2 minutes.*

10. The Attunement is complete. Perform the finishing steps.

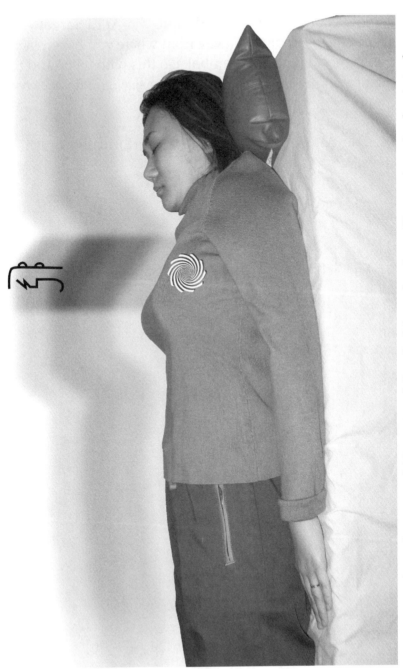

(Photo 31) Place the Mental/Emotional Symbol into the Aura Target Area in the Astral

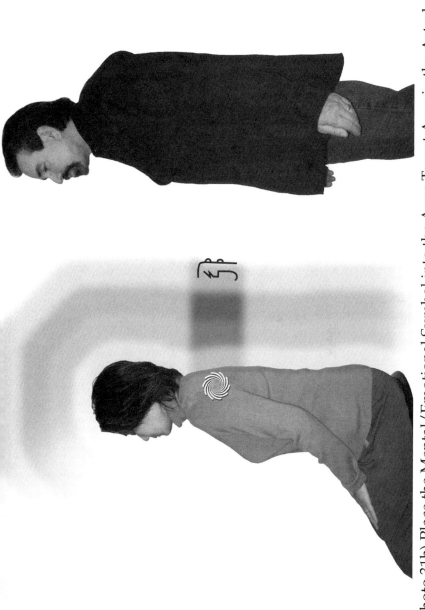

(Photo 31b) Place the Mental/Emotional Symbol into the Aura Target Area in the Astral Layer that is aligned with the fourth Chakra.

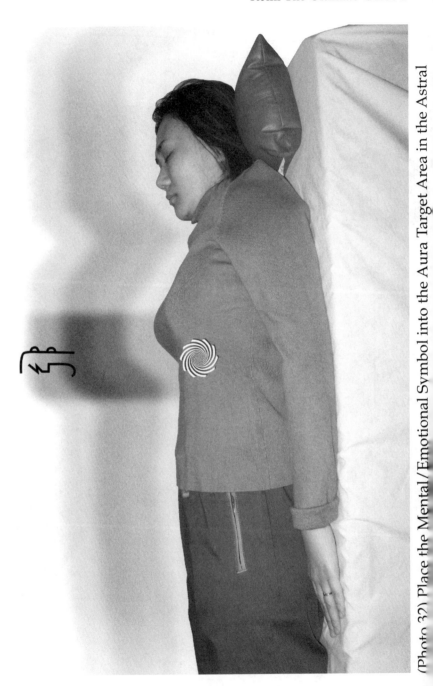

(Photo 32) Place the Mental/Emotional Symbol into the Aura Target Area in the Astral

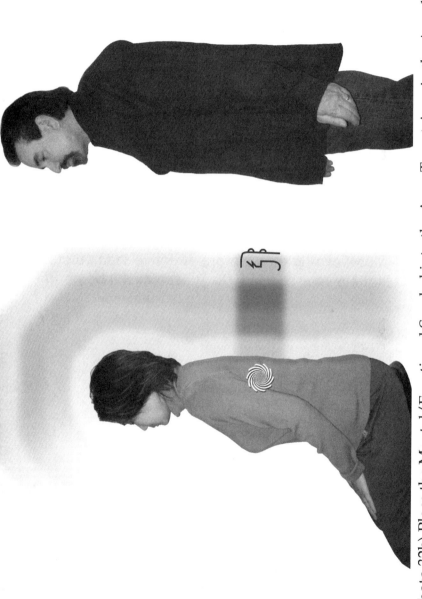

(Photo 32b) Place the Mental/Emotional Symbol into the Aura Target Area in the Astral Layer that is aligned with the third Chakra.

Moral examples are more effective than edicts.
If the leader is good, the followers will be good
and follow the example.

-Confucius

Reiki Aura Attunement
Insecurity

Intent

Insecurity usually creates low self-esteem. If you know what the insecurity issue is, use that as the Root Intent, but if not known, use Generic Intent.

1. You have prepared for the Aura Attunement.

2. You are in the proper position to either perform the Attunement on yourself or another person in a quiet area where you will not be disturbed.

3. State the intent for the Aura Attunement silently to yourself before you begin. At this time, you can also ask for guidance during the Attunement. *Step should only take a few seconds.*

4. If you are a Reiki Master, place the Master Symbol into the palms of your hands, then activate it. ***2nd Level Healers omit this step.***

5. Now place the Power Symbol into the palms of your hands and activate it.

6. Next place the Mental/Emotional Symbol into the Aura Target Area in the Astral Layer that is aligned with the fourth Chakra as shown (Photos 33 and 33b), then activate the symbol. *Step should only take 15 seconds.*

7. Now channel Reiki directly into the Aura Target Area about one to two inches away from where you have placed the Mental/Emotional Symbol. Do this with focus and the intent you have decided upon. *Step should only take about 2 minutes.*

8. Next, place the Mental/Emotional Symbol into the second Aura Target Area in the Astral Layer that is aligned with the sixth Chakra as shown (Photos 34 and 34b), then activate the symbol. *Step should only take 15 seconds.*

9. Now channel Reiki directly into the Aura Target Area about one to two inches away from where you have placed the Mental/Emotional Symbol. Do this with focus and the intent you have decided upon. *Step should only take about 2 minutes.*

10. The Attunement is complete. Perform the finishing steps.

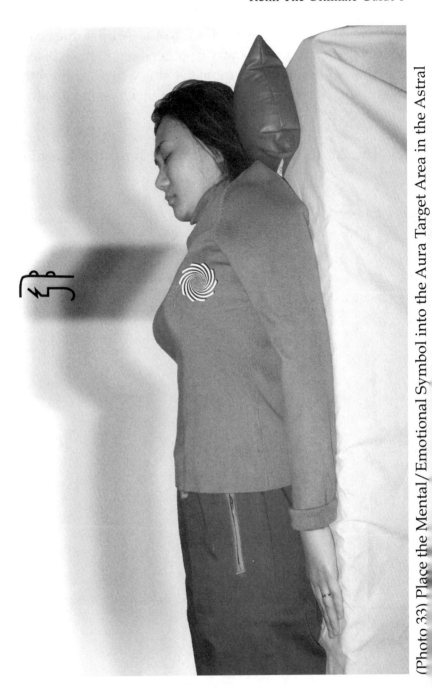

(Photo.33) Place the Mental/Emotional Symbol into the Aura Target Area in the Astral

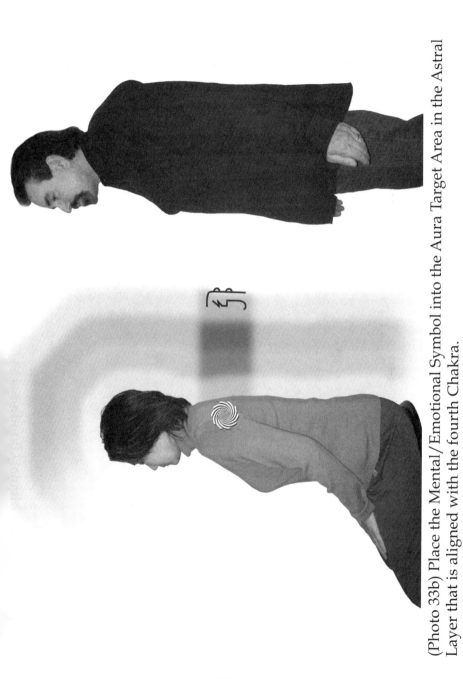

(Photo 33b) Place the Mental/Emotional Symbol into the Aura Target Area in the Astral Layer that is aligned with the fourth Chakra.

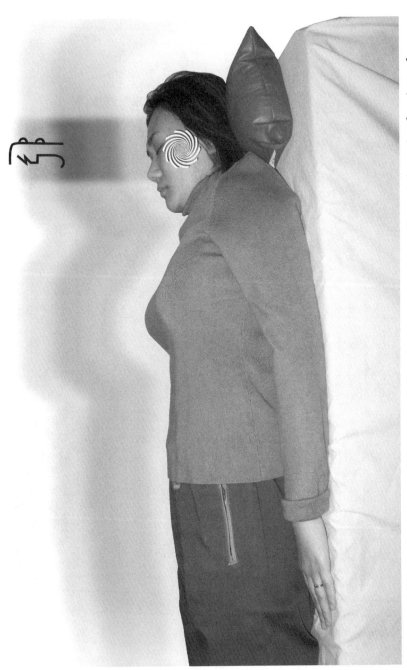

(Photo 34) Place the Mental/Emotional Symbol into the Aura Target Area in the Astral

(Photo 34b) Place the Mental/Emotional Symbol into the Aura Target Area in the Astral Layer that is aligned with the sixth Chakra.

217

Forget injuries, never forget kindnesses.
-Confucius

Reiki Aura Attunement
Insomnia

Intent

Insomnia is difficult to use Root Intent because it can manifest from many mental or emotional issues at the same time. Just use Generic Intent for this Attunement.

1. You have prepared for the Aura Attunement.

2. You are in the proper position to either perform the Attunement on yourself or another person in a quiet area where you will not be disturbed.

3. State the intent for the Aura Attunement silently to yourself before you begin. At this time, you can also ask for guidance during the Attunement. *Step should only take a few seconds.*

4. If you are a Reiki Master, place the Master Symbol into the palms of your hands, then activate it. **2nd Level Healers omit this step.**

5. Now place the Power Symbol into the palms of your hands and activate it.

6. Next place the Mental/Emotional Symbol into the Aura Target Area in the Astral Layer that is aligned with the second Chakra as shown (Photos 35 and 35b), then activate the symbol. *Step should only take 15 seconds.*

7. Now channel Reiki directly into the Aura Target Area about one to two inches away from where you have placed the Mental/Emotional Symbol. Do this with focus and the intent you have decided upon. *Step should only take about 2 minutes.*

8. Next, place the Mental/Emotional Symbol into the second Aura Target Area in the Astral Layer that is aligned with the third Chakra as shown (Photos 36 and 36b), then activate the symbol. *Step should only take 15 seconds.*

9. Now channel Reiki directly into the Aura Target Area about one to two inches away from where you have placed the Mental/Emotional Symbol. Do this with focus and the intent you have decided upon. *Step should only take about 2 minutes.*

10. The Attunement is complete. Perform the finishing steps.

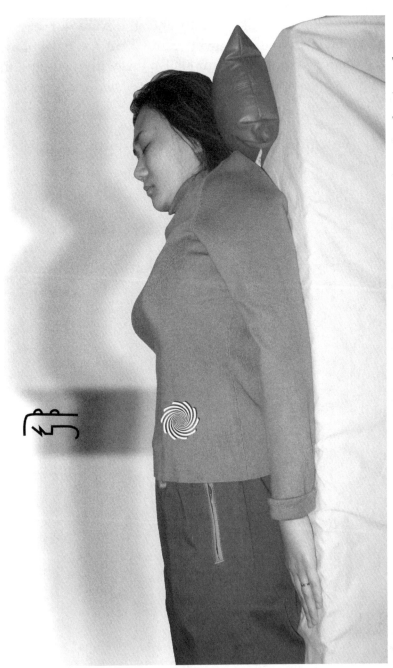

(Photo 35) Place the Mental/Emotional Symbol into the Aura Target Area in the Astral

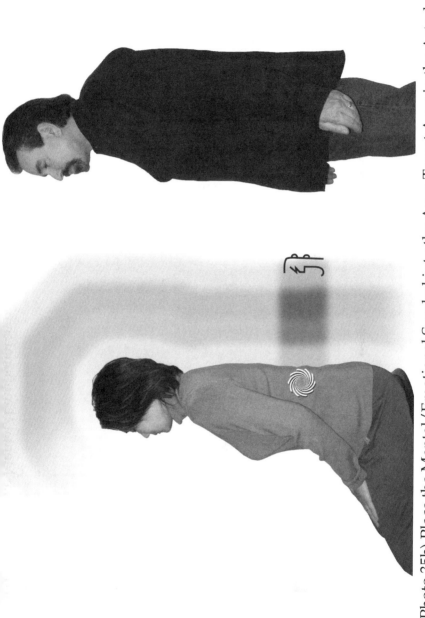

(Photo 35b) Place the Mental/Emotional Symbol into the Aura Target Area in the Astral Layer that is aligned with the second Chakra.

223

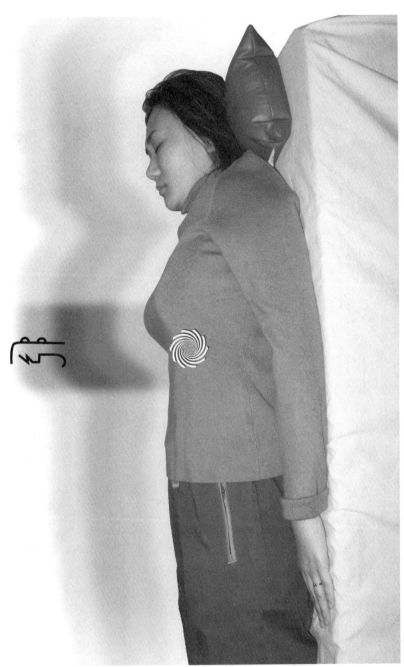

(Photo 36) Place the Mental/Emotional Symbol into the Aura Target Area in the Astral

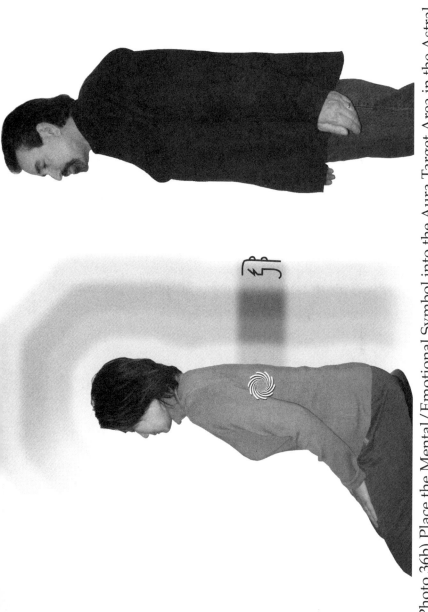

(Photo 36b) Place the Mental/Emotional Symbol into the Aura Target Area in the Astral Layer that is aligned with the third Chakra.

225

If you have faults, do not fear self-improvement.
-Confucius

Reiki Aura Attunement
Jealousy

twenty three

Intent

Use Root Intent for this Attunement if the cause of the jealousy is known, but if not known, use Generic Intent.

1. You have prepared for the Aura Attunement.

2. You are in the proper position to either perform the Attunement on yourself or another person in a quiet area where you will not be disturbed.

3. State the intent for the Aura Attunement silently to yourself before you begin. At this time, you can also ask for guidance during the Attunement. *Step should only take a few seconds.*

4. If you are a Reiki Master, place the Master Symbol into the palms of your hands, then activate it. **2nd Level Healers omit this step.**

5. Now place the Power Symbol into the palms of your hands and activate it.

6. Next place the Mental/Emotional Symbol into the Aura Target Area in the Astral Layer that is aligned with the sixth Chakra as shown (Photos 37 and 37b), then activate the symbol. *Step should only take 15 seconds.*

7. Now channel Reiki directly into the Aura Target Area about one to two inches away from where you have placed the Mental/Emotional Symbol. Do this with focus and the intent you have decided upon. *Step should only take about 2 minutes.*

8. Next, place the Mental/Emotional Symbol into the second Aura Target Area in the Astral Layer that is aligned with the third Chakra as shown (Photos 38 and 38b), then activate the symbol. *Step should only take 15 seconds.*

9. Now channel Reiki directly into the Aura Target Area about one to two inches away from where you have placed the Mental/Emotional Symbol. Do this with focus and the intent you have decided upon. *Step should only take about 2 minutes.*

10. The Attunement is complete. Perform the finishing steps.

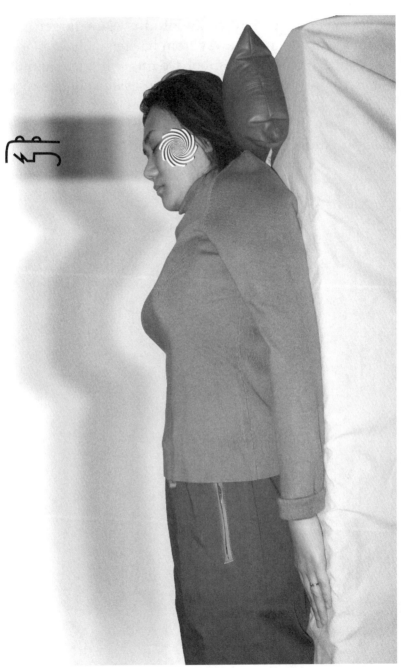

(Photo 37) Place the Mental/Emotional Symbol into the Aura Target Area in the Astral

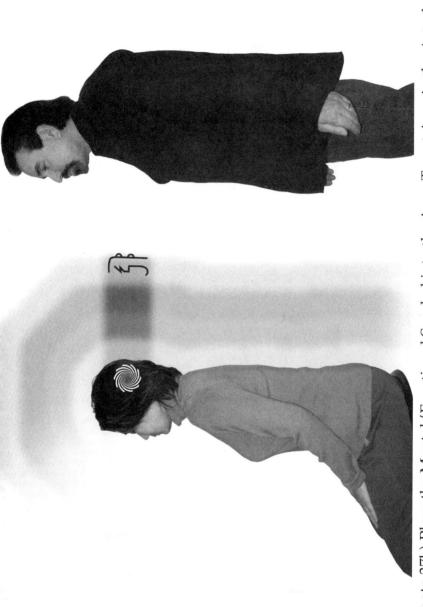

(Photo 37b) Place the Mental/Emotional Symbol into the Aura Target Area in the Astral Layer that is aligned with the sixth Chakra.

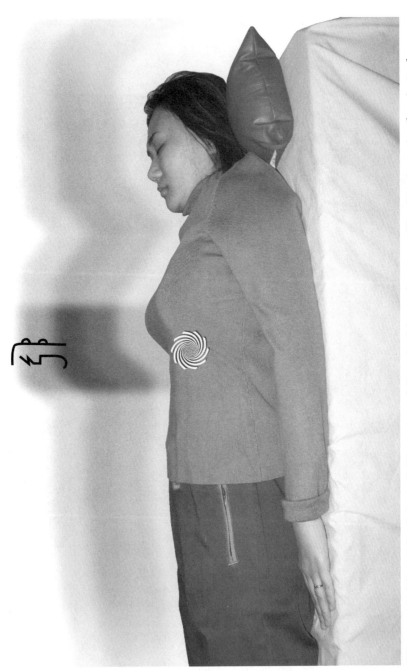

(Photo 38) Place the Mental/Emotional Symbol into the Aura Target Area in the Astral

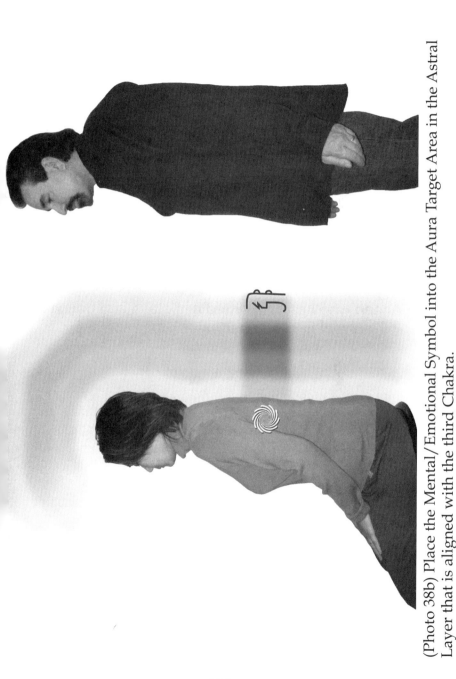

(Photo 38b) Place the Mental/Emotional Symbol into the Aura Target Area in the Astral Layer that is aligned with the third Chakra.

233

A man who has committed a mistake and doesn't correct it, is committing another mistake.

-Confucius

Reiki Aura Attunement
Love Issues

twenty
four

Intent

For this Attunement you really need to know what the exact love issue is that is causing the problem and use it as the Root Intent for this Attunement. Examples: love issues with ex-partners, children, relatives, etc.

1. You have prepared for the Aura Attunement.

2. You are in the proper position to either perform the Attunement on yourself or another person in a quiet area where you will not be disturbed.

3. State the intent for the Aura Attunement silently to yourself before you begin. At this time, you can also ask for guidance during the Attunement. *Step should only take a few seconds.*

4. If you are a Reiki Master, place the Master Symbol into the palms of your hands, then activate it. ***2nd Level Healers omit this step.***

5. Now place the Power Symbol into the palms of your hands and activate it.

6. Next place the Mental/Emotional Symbol into the Aura Target Area in the Astral Layer that is aligned with the fourth Chakra as shown (Photos 39 and 39b), then activate the symbol. *Step should only take 15 seconds.*

7. Now channel Reiki directly into the Aura Target Area about one to two inches away from where you have placed the Mental/Emotional Symbol. Do this with focus and the intent you have decided upon. *Step should only take about 2 minutes.*

8. Next, place the Mental/Emotional Symbol into the second Aura Target Area in the Astral Layer that is aligned with the seventh Chakra as shown (Photos 40 and 40b), then activate the symbol. *Step should only take 15 seconds.*

9. Now channel Reiki directly into the Aura Target Area about one to two inches away from where you have placed the Mental/Emotional Symbol. Do this with focus and the intent you have decided upon. *Step should only take about 2 minutes.*

10. The Attunement is complete. Perform the finishing steps.

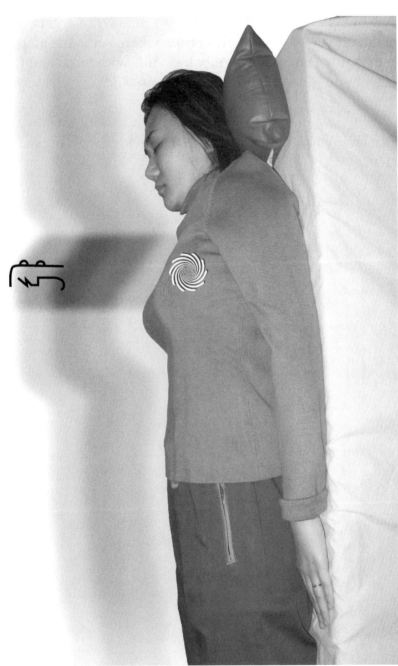

(Photo 39) Place the Mental / Emotional Symbol into the Aura Target Area in the Astral

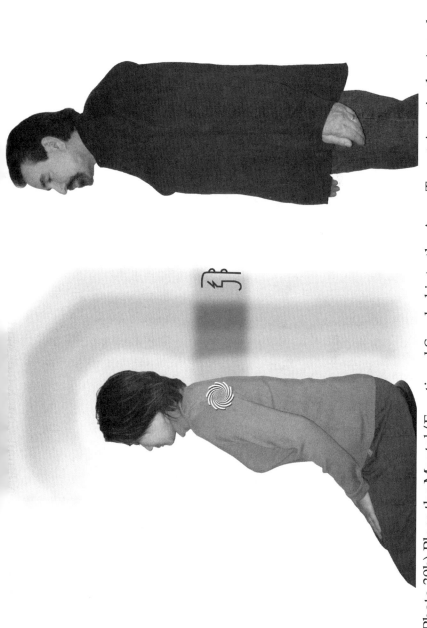

(Photo 39b) Place the Mental/Emotional Symbol into the Aura Target Area in the Astral Layer that is aligned with the fourth Chakra.

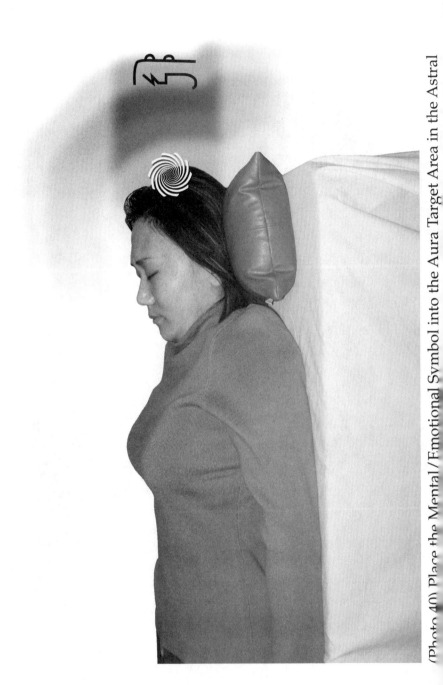

(Photo 40) Place the Mental/Emotional Symbol into the Aura Target Area in the Astral

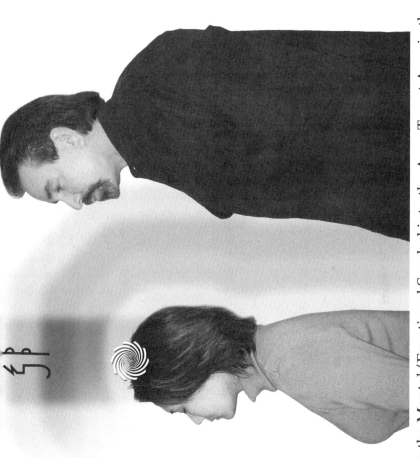

(Photo 40b) Place the Mental/Emotional Symbol into the Aura Target Area in the Astral Layer that is aligned with the seventh Chakra.

I hear, I know. I see, I remember. I do, I understand.
-Confucius

Reiki Aura Attunement
Memory Issues

twenty
five

Intent

Generic Intent should be used for this Attunement because many emotional and mental issues can combine to cause memory loss. You can use Root Intent if the exact cause is known.

1. You have prepared for the Aura Attunement.

2. You are in the proper position to either perform the Attunement on yourself or another person in a quiet area where you will not be disturbed.

3. State the intent for the Aura Attunement silently to yourself before you begin. At this time, you can also ask for guidance during the Attunement. *Step should only take a few seconds.*

4. If you are a Reiki Master, place the Master Symbol into the palms of your hands, then activate it. ***2nd Level Healers omit this step.***

5. Now place the Power Symbol into the palms of your hands and activate it.

6. Next place the Mental/Emotional Symbol into the Aura Target Area in the Astral Layer that is aligned with the seventh Chakra as shown (Photos 41 and 41b), then activate the symbol. *Step should only take 15 seconds.*

7. Now channel Reiki directly into the Aura Target Area about one to two inches away from where you have placed the Mental/Emotional Symbol. Do this with focus and the intent you have decided upon. *Step should only take about 2 minutes.*

8. Next, place the Mental/Emotional Symbol into the second Aura Target Area in the Astral Layer that is aligned with the sixth Chakra as shown (Photos 42 and 42b), then activate the symbol. *Step should only take 15 seconds.*

9. Now channel Reiki directly into the Aura Target Area about one to two inches away from where you have placed the Mental/Emotional Symbol. Do this with focus and the intent you have decided upon. *Step should only take about 2 minutes.*

10. The Attunement is complete. Perform the finishing steps.

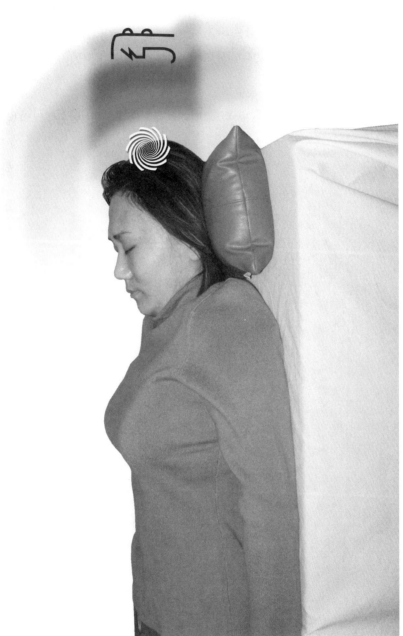

(Photo 41) Place the Mental / Emotional Symbol into the Aura Target Area in the Astral

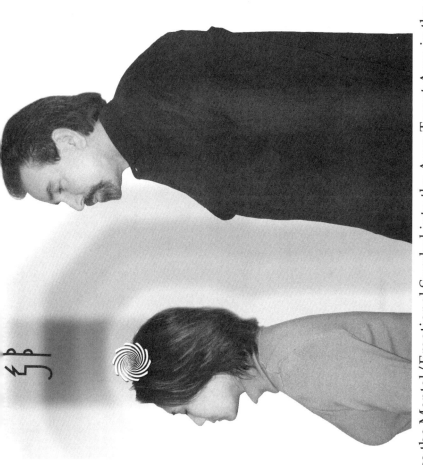

(Photo 41b) Place the Mental/Emotional Symbol into the Aura Target Area in the Astral Layer that is aligned with the seventh Chakra.

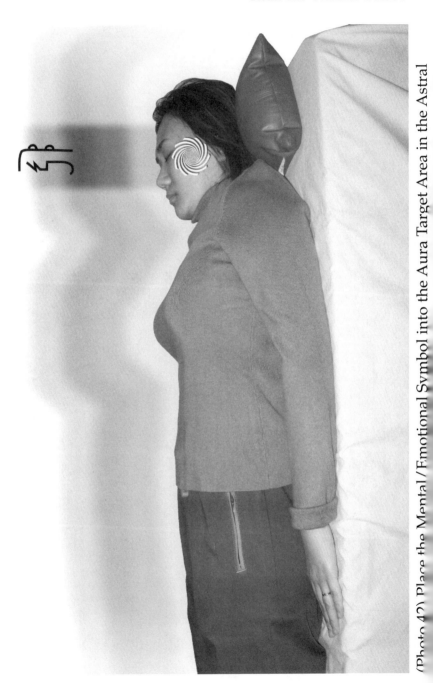

(Photo 42) Place the Mental/Emotional Symbol into the Aura Target Area in the Astral

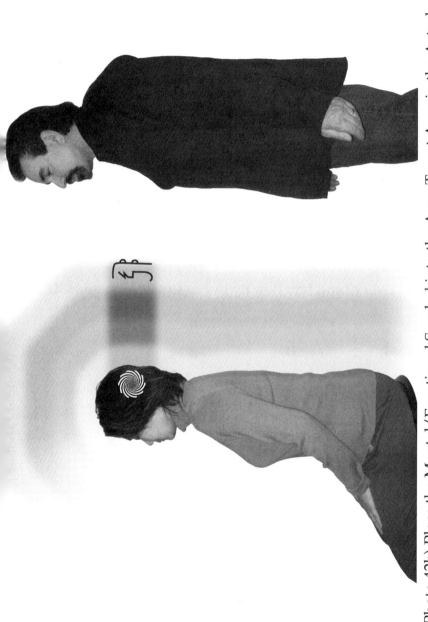

(Photo 42b) Place the Mental/Emotional Symbol into the Aura Target Area in the Astral Layer that is aligned with the sixth Chakra.

Everything has beauty but not everyone sees it.
-Confucius

Reiki Aura Attunement
Mental Blocks

Intent

Use Root Intent for this Attunement if the cause of the mental block is known, but if mental block is not known, use Generic Intent.

1. You have prepared for the Aura Attunement.

2. You are in the proper position to either perform the Attunement on yourself or another person in a quiet area where you will not be disturbed.

3. State the intent for the Aura Attunement silently to yourself before you begin. At this time, you can also ask for guidance during the Attunement. *Step should only take a few seconds.*

4. If you are a Reiki Master, place the Master Symbol into the palms of your hands, then activate it. **2nd Level Healers omit this step.**

5. Now place the Power Symbol into the palms of your hands and activate it.

6. Next place the Mental/Emotional Symbol into the Aura Target Area in the Astral Layer that is aligned with the sixth Chakra as shown (Photos 43 and 43b), then activate the symbol. *Step should only take 15 seconds.*

7. Now channel Reiki directly into the Aura Target Area about one to two inches away from where you have placed the Mental/Emotional Symbol. Do this with focus and the intent you have decided upon. *Step should only take about 2 minutes.*

8. Next, place the Mental/Emotional Symbol into the second Aura Target Area in the Astral Layer that is aligned with the seventh Chakra as shown (Photos 44 and 44b), then activate the symbol. *Step should only take 15 seconds.*

9. Now channel Reiki directly into the Aura Target Area about one to two inches away from where you have placed the Mental/Emotional Symbol. Do this with focus and the intent you have decided upon. *Step should only take about 2 minutes.*

10. The Attunement is complete. Perform the finishing steps.

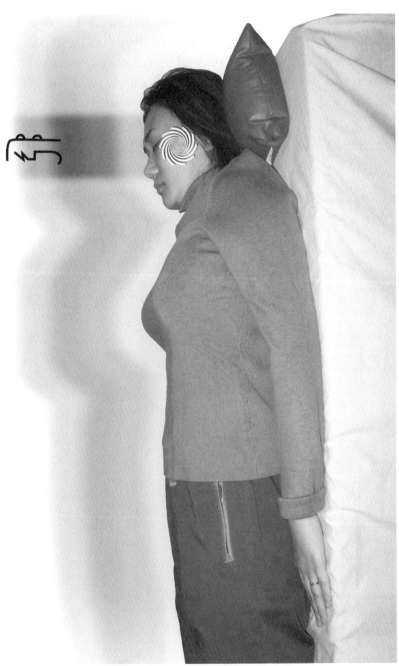

(Photo 43) Place the Mental/Emotional Symbol into the Aura Target Area in the Astral

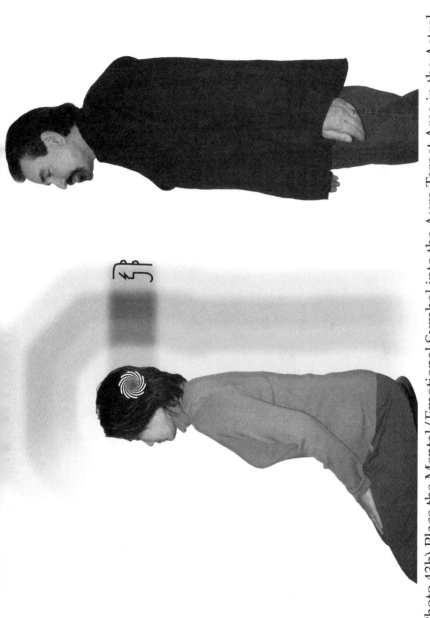

(Photo 43b) Place the Mental/Emotional Symbol into the Aura Target Area in the Astral Layer that is aligned with the sixth Chakra.

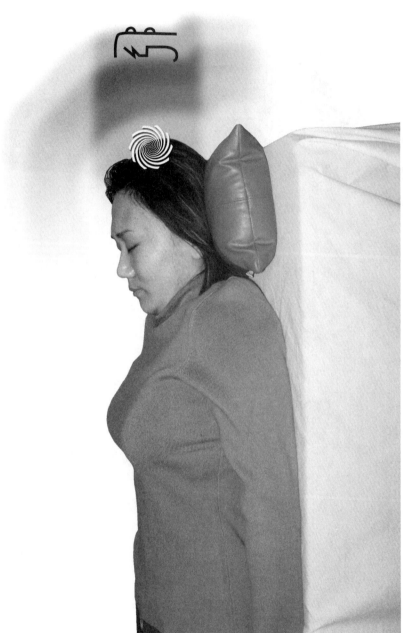

(Photo 44) Place the Mental/Emotional Symbol into the Aura Target Area in the Astral

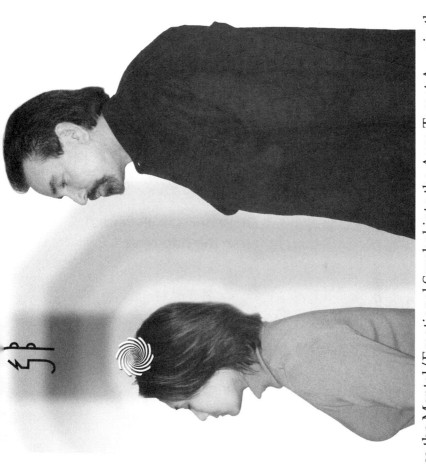

(Photo 44b) Place the Mental/Emotional Symbol into the Aura Target Area in the Astral Layer that is aligned with the seventh Chakra.

It is better to light one small candle than to curse the darkness.

-Confucius

Reiki Aura Attunement
Money Issues

twenty
seven

Intent

Mental and emotional money issues are usually always known, so use Root Intent for this Attunement. Generic Intent can also be used.

1. You have prepared for the Aura Attunement.

2. You are in the proper position to either perform the Attunement on yourself or another person in a quiet area where you will not be disturbed.

3. State the intent for the Aura Attunement silently to yourself before you begin. At this time, you can also ask for guidance during the Attunement. *Step should only take a few seconds.*

4. If you are a Reiki Master, place the Master Symbol into the palms of your hands, then activate it. ***2nd Level Healers omit this step.***

5. Now place the Power Symbol into the palms of your hands and activate it.

6. Next place the Mental/Emotional Symbol into the Aura Target Area in the Astral Layer that is aligned with the fifth Chakra as shown (Photos 45 and 45b), then activate the symbol. *Step should only take 15 seconds.*

7. Now channel Reiki directly into the Aura Target Area about one to two inches away from where you have placed the Mental/Emotional Symbol. Do this with focus and the intent you have decided upon. *Step should only take about 2 minutes.*

8. Next, place the Mental/Emotional Symbol into the second Aura Target Area in the Astral Layer that is aligned with the third Chakra as shown (Photos 46 and 46b), then activate the symbol. *Step should only take 15 seconds.*

9. Now channel Reiki directly into the Aura Target Area about one to two inches away from where you have placed the Mental/Emotional Symbol. Do this with focus and the intent you have decided upon. *Step should only take about 2 minutes.*

10. The Attunement is complete. Perform the finishing steps.

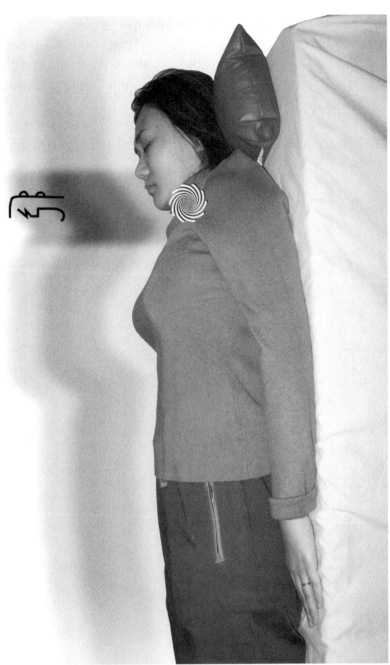

(Photo 45) Place the Mental/Emotional Symbol into the Aura Target Area in the Astral

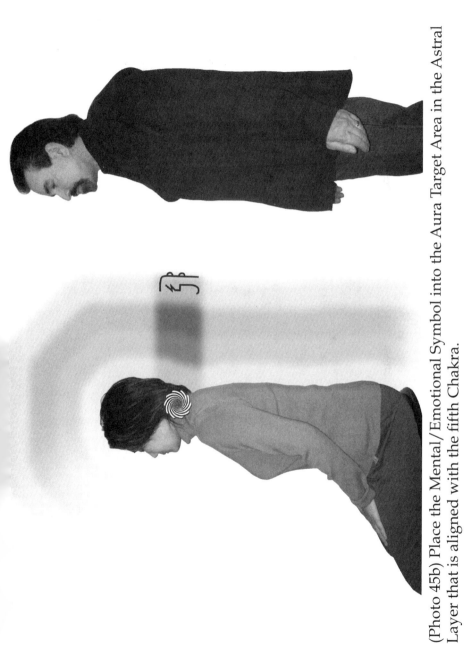

(Photo 45b) Place the Mental/Emotional Symbol into the Aura Target Area in the Astral Layer that is aligned with the fifth Chakra.

263

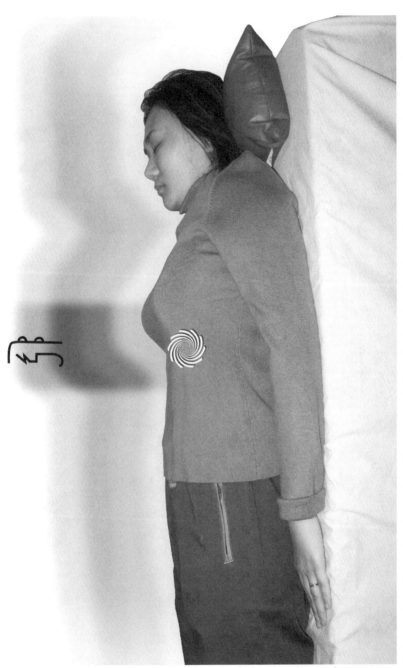

(Photo 46) Place the Mental/Emotional Symbol into the Aura Target Area in the Astral

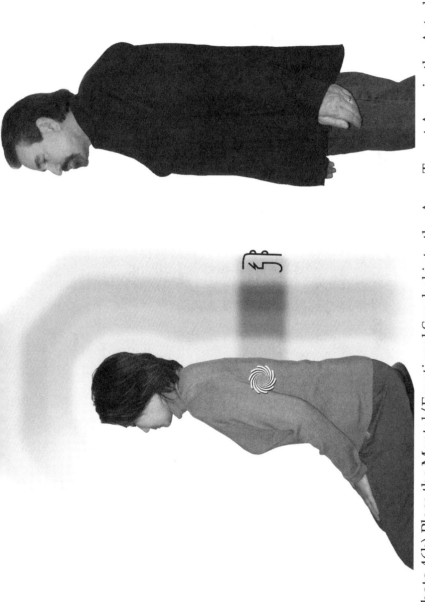

(Photo 46b) Place the Mental/Emotional Symbol into the Aura Target Area in the Astral Layer that is aligned with the third Chakra.

265

**To be wronged is nothing
unless you continue to remember it.**
                                           -Confucius

Reiki Aura Attunement
Obsessive Issues

Intent

An obsessive issue is usually known, so use Root Intent. Generic Intent is not recommend for this Aura Attunement.

1. You have prepared for the Aura Attunement.

2. You are in the proper position to either perform the Attunement on yourself or another person in a quiet area where you will not be disturbed.

3. State the intent for the Aura Attunement silently to yourself before you begin. At this time, you can also ask for guidance during the Attunement. *Step should only take a few seconds.*

4. If you are a Reiki Master, place the Master Symbol into the palms of your hands, then activate it. **2nd Level Healers omit this step.**

5. Now place the Power Symbol into the palms of your hands and activate it.

6. Next place the Mental/Emotional Symbol into the Aura Target Area in the Astral Layer that is aligned with the first Chakra as shown (Photos 47 and 47b), then activate the symbol. *Step should only take 15 seconds.*

7. Now channel Reiki directly into the Aura Target Area about one to two inches away from where you have placed the Mental/Emotional Symbol. Do this with focus and the intent you have decided upon. *Step should only take about 2 minutes.*

8. Next, place the Mental/Emotional Symbol into the second Aura Target Area in the Astral Layer that is aligned with the sixth Chakra as shown (Photos 48 and 48b), then activate the symbol. *Step should only take 15 seconds.*

9. Now channel Reiki directly into the Aura Target Area about one to two inches away from where you have placed the Mental/Emotional Symbol. Do this with focus and the intent you have decided upon. *Step should only take about 2 minutes.*

10. The Attunement is complete. Perform the finishing steps.

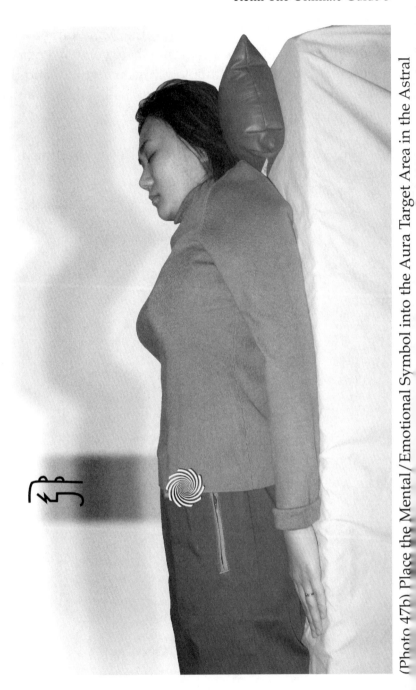

(Photo 47b) Place the Mental/Emotional Symbol into the Aura Target Area in the Astral

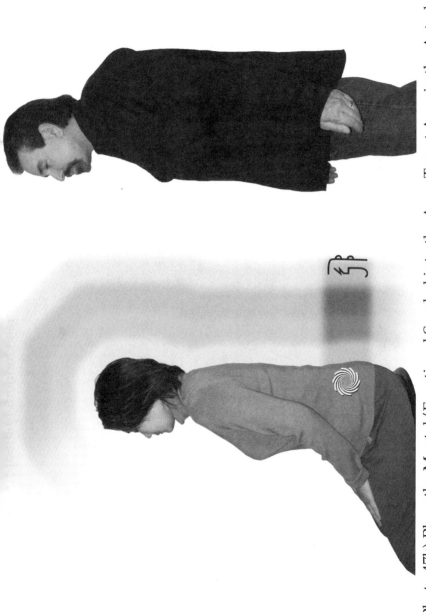

(Photo 47b) Place the Mental/Emotional Symbol into the Aura Target Area in the Astral Layer that is aligned with the first Chakra.

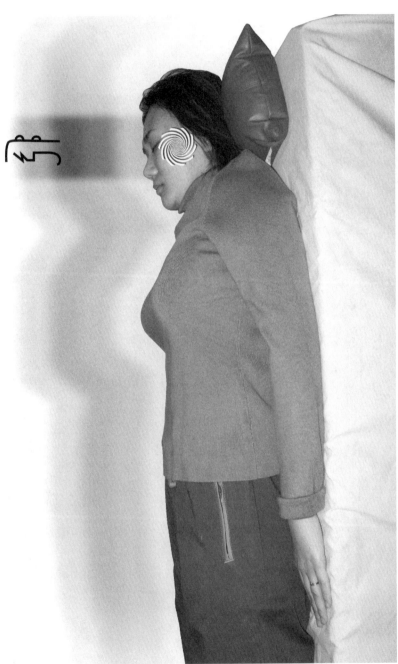

(Photo 48) Place the Mental/Emotional Symbol into the Aura Target Area in the Astral

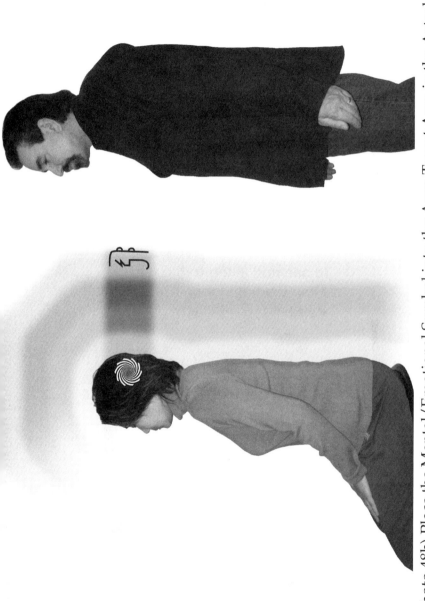

(Photo 48b) Place the Mental/Emotional Symbol into the Aura Target Area in the Astral Layer that is aligned with the sixth Chakra.

To see and listen to the wicked
is already the beginning of wickedness.

-Confucius

Reiki Aura Attunement
Panic

twenty
nine

Intent

Use Root Intent if the exact mental or emotional issue is known, but if not known, use Generic Intent.

1. You have prepared for the Aura Attunement.

2. You are in the proper position to either perform the Attunement on yourself or another person in a quiet area where you will not be disturbed.

3. State the intent for the Aura Attunement silently to yourself before you begin. At this time, you can also ask for guidance during the Attunement. *Step should only take a few seconds.*

4. If you are a Reiki Master, place the Master Symbol into the palms of your hands, then activate it. **2nd Level Healers omit this step.**

5. Now place the Power Symbol into the palms of your hands and activate it.

6. Next place the Mental/Emotional Symbol into the Aura Target Area in the Astral Layer that is aligned with the second Chakra as shown (Photos 49 and 49b), then activate the symbol. *Step should only take 15 seconds.*

7. Now channel Reiki directly into the Aura Target Area about one to two inches away from where you have placed the Mental/Emotional Symbol. Do this with focus and the intent you have decided upon. *Step should only take about 2 minutes.*

8. Next, place the Mental/Emotional Symbol into the second Aura Target Area in the Astral Layer that is aligned with the sixth Chakra as shown (Photos 50 and 50b), then activate the symbol. *Step should only take 15 seconds.*

9. Now channel Reiki directly into the Aura Target Area about one to two inches away from where you have placed the Mental/Emotional Symbol. Do this with focus and the intent you have decided upon. *Step should only take about 2 minutes.*

10. The Attunement is complete. Perform the finishing steps.

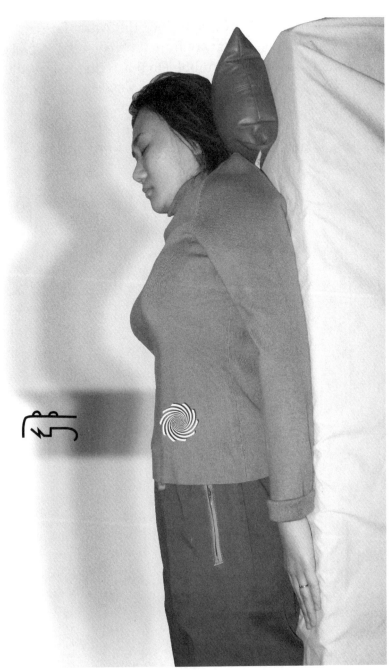

(Photo 49) Place the Mental/Emotional Symbol into the Aura Target Area in the Astral

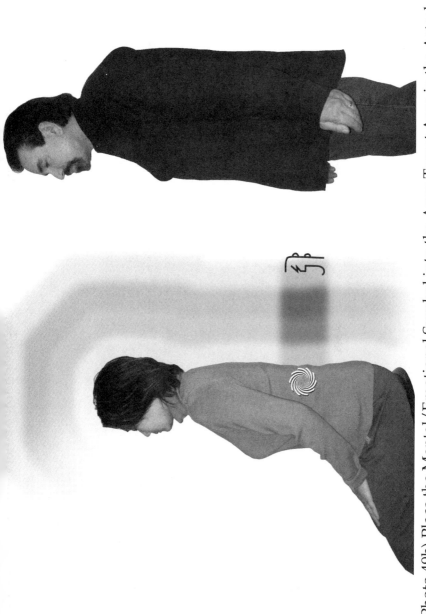

(Photo 49b) Place the Mental/Emotional Symbol into the Aura Target Area in the Astral Layer that is aligned with the second Chakra.

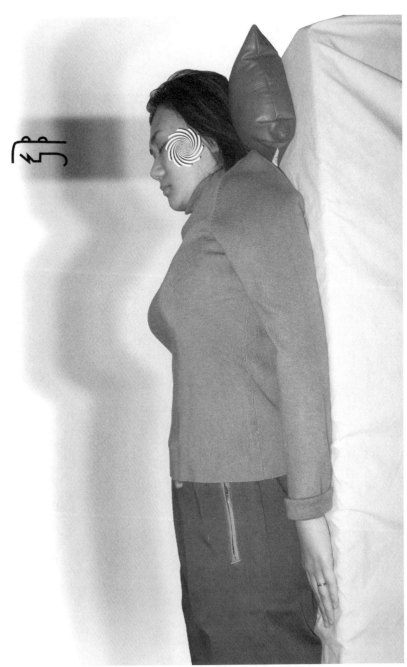

(Photo 50) Place the Mental / Emotional Symbol into the Aura Target Area in the Astral

(Photo 50b) Place the Mental/Emotional Symbol into the Aura Target Area in the Astral Layer that is aligned with the sixth Chakra.

And remember, no matter where you go, there you are.

-Confucius

Reiki Aura Attunement Phobias

Intent

The Phobia should be known for the Root Intent. You can use Generic Intent, but it is not really desirable with this Attunement.

1. You have prepared for the Aura Attunement.

2. You are in the proper position to either perform the Attunement on yourself or another person in a quiet area where you will not be disturbed.

3. State the intent for the Aura Attunement silently to yourself before you begin. At this time, you can also ask for guidance during the Attunement. *Step should only take a few seconds.*

4. If you are a Reiki Master, place the Master Symbol into the palms of your hands, then activate it. **2nd Level Healers omit this step.**

5. Now place the Power Symbol into the palms of your hands and activate it.

6. Next place the Mental/Emotional Symbol into the Aura Target Area in the Astral Layer that is aligned with the seventh Chakra as shown (Photos 51 and 51b), then activate the symbol. *Step should only take 15 seconds.*

7. Now channel Reiki directly into the Aura Target Area about one to two inches away from where you have placed the Mental/Emotional Symbol. Do this with focus and the intent you have decided upon. *Step should only take about 2 minutes.*

8. Next, place the Mental/Emotional Symbol into the second Aura Target Area in the Astral Layer that is aligned with the first Chakra as shown (Photos 52 and 52b), then activate the symbol. *Step should only take 15 seconds.*

9. Now channel Reiki directly into the Aura Target Area about one to two inches away from where you have placed the Mental/Emotional Symbol. Do this with focus and the intent you have decided upon. *Step should only take about 2 minutes.*

10. The Attunement is complete. Perform the finishing steps.

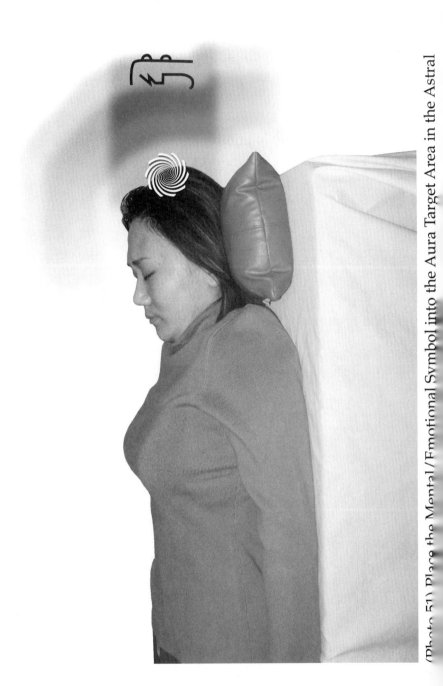

(Photo 51) Place the Mental/Emotional Symbol into the Aura Target Area in the Astral

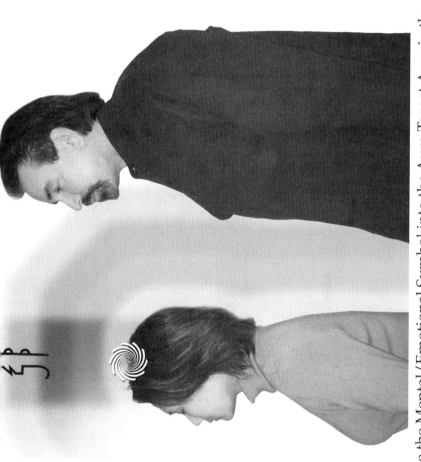

(Photo 51b) Place the Mental/Emotional Symbol into the Aura Target Area in the Astral Layer that is aligned with the seventh Chakra.

287

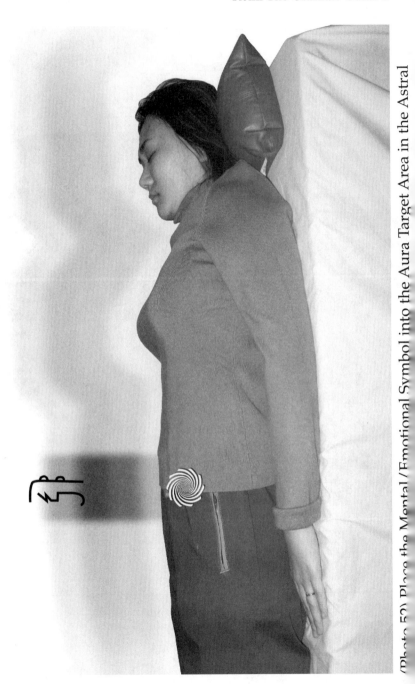

(Photo 52) Place the Mental/Emotional Symbol into the Aura Target Area in the Astral

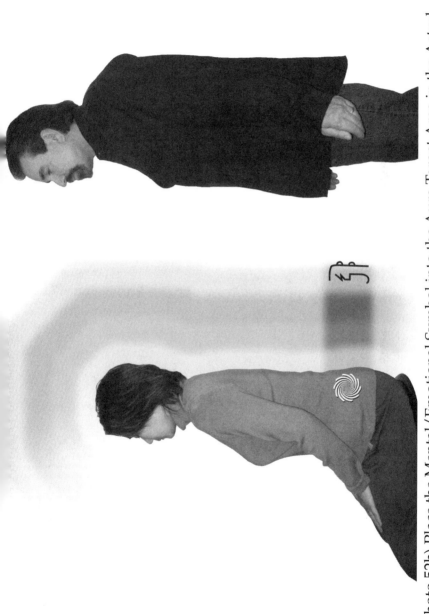

(Photo 52b) Place the Mental/Emotional Symbol into the Aura Target Area in the Astral Layer that is aligned with the first Chakra.

If we don't know life, how can we know death?
-Confucius

Reiki Aura Attunement
Psychological Issues

Intent

The Psychological Issue should be known for the Root
Intent. You can use Generic Intent, but it is not recommended with this Attunement.

1. You have prepared for the Aura Attunement.

2. You are in the proper position to either perform the Attunement on yourself or another person in a quiet area where you will not be disturbed.

3. State the intent for the Aura Attunement silently to yourself before you begin. At this time, you can also ask for guidance during the Attunement. *Step should only take a few seconds.*

4. If you are a Reiki Master, place the Master Symbol into the palms of your hands, then activate it. **2nd Level Healers omit this step.**

5. Now place the Power Symbol into the palms of your hands and activate it.

6. Next place the Mental/Emotional Symbol into the Aura Target Area in the Astral Layer that is aligned with the sixth Chakra as shown (Photos 53 and 53b), then activate the symbol. *Step should only take 15 seconds.*

7. Now channel Reiki directly into the Aura Target Area about one to two inches away from where you have placed the Mental/Emotional Symbol. Do this with focus and the intent you have decided upon. *Step should only take about 2 minutes.*

8. Next, place the Mental/Emotional Symbol into the second Aura Target Area in the Astral Layer that is aligned with the first Chakra as shown (Photos 54 and 54b), then activate the symbol. *Step should only take 15 seconds.*

9. Now channel Reiki directly into the Aura Target Area about one to two inches away from where you have placed the Mental/Emotional Symbol. Do this with focus and the intent you have decided upon. *Step should only take about 2 minutes.*

10. The Attunement is complete. Perform the finishing steps.

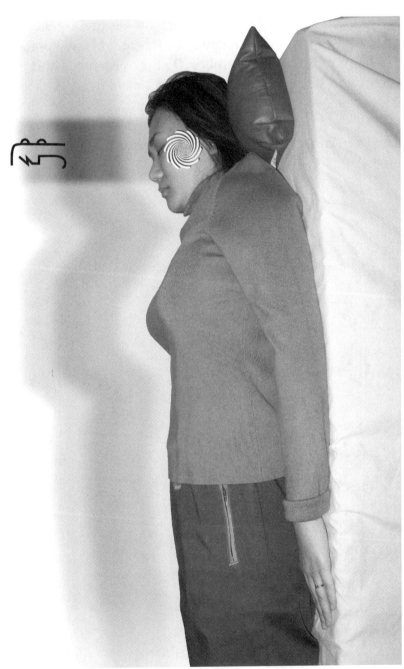

Photo 52) Place the Mental / Emotional Symbol into the Aura Target Area in the Astral

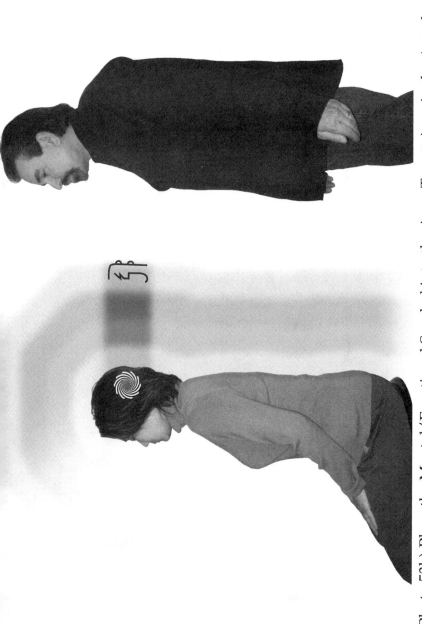

(Photo 53b) Place the Mental/Emotional Symbol into the Aura Target Area in the Astral Layer that is aligned with the sixth Chakra.

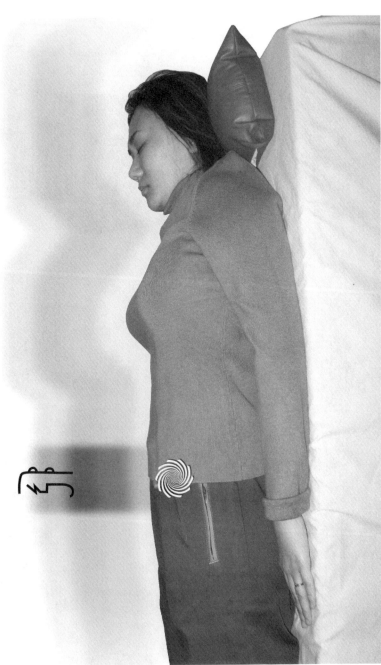

(Photo 54) Place the Mental/Emotional Symbol into the Aura Target Area in the Astral

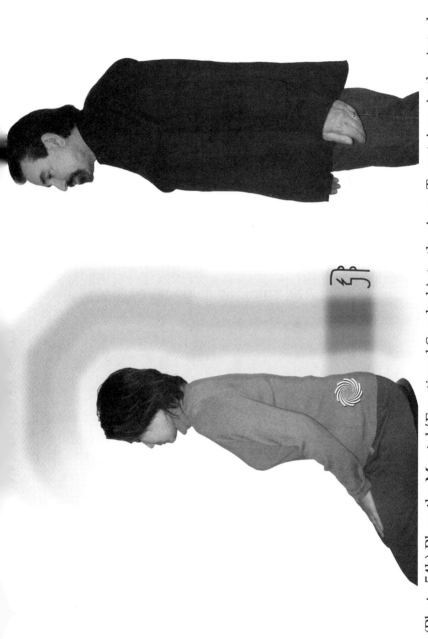

(Photo 54b) Place the Mental/Emotional Symbol into the Aura Target Area in the Astral Layer that is aligned with the first Chakra.

The cautious seldom err.

-Confucius

Reiki Aura Attunement
Sexual Issues

thirty
two

Intent

Most of the time sexual mental and emotional issues are private, so use Generic Intent for this one. But, you can use Root Intent with yourself or with another person who is comfortable with disclosing the issue.

1. You have prepared for the Aura Attunement.

2. You are in the proper position to either perform the Attunement on yourself or another person in a quiet area where you will not be disturbed.

3. State the intent for the Aura Attunement silently to yourself before you begin. At this time, you can also ask for guidance during the Attunement. *Step should only take a few seconds.*

4. If you are a Reiki Master, place the Master Symbol into the palms of your hands, then activate it. **2nd Level Healers omit this step.**

5. Now place the Power Symbol into the palms of your hands and activate it.

6. Next place the Mental/Emotional Symbol into the Aura Target Area in the Astral Layer that is aligned with the third Chakra as shown (Photos 55 and 55b), then activate the symbol. *Step should only take 15 seconds.*

7. Now channel Reiki directly into the Aura Target Area about one to two inches away from where you have placed the Mental/Emotional Symbol. Do this with focus and the intent you have decided upon. *Step should only take about 2 minutes.*

8. Next, place the Mental/Emotional Symbol into the second Aura Target Area in the Astral Layer that is aligned with the second Chakra as shown (Photos 56 and 56b), then activate the symbol. *Step should only take 15 seconds.*

9. Now channel Reiki directly into the Aura Target Area about one to two inches away from where you have placed the Mental/Emotional Symbol. Do this with focus and the intent you have decided upon. *Step should only take about 2 minutes.*

10. The Attunement is complete. Perform the finishing steps.

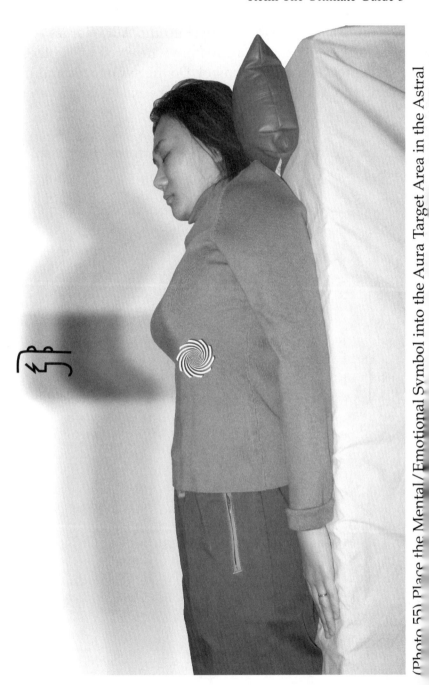

(Photo 55) Place the Mental/Emotional Symbol into the Aura Target Area in the Astral

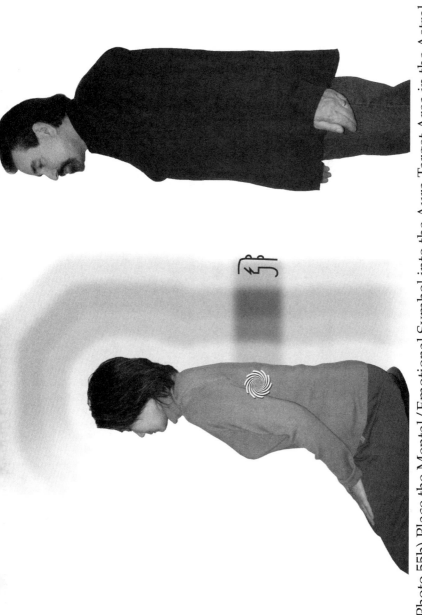

(Photo 55b) Place the Mental/Emotional Symbol into the Aura Target Area in the Astral Layer that is aligned with the third Chakra.

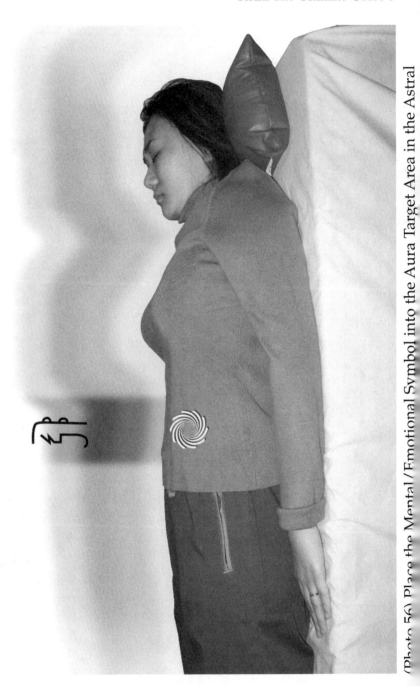

(Photo 56) Place the Mental/Emotional Symbol into the Aura Target Area in the Astral

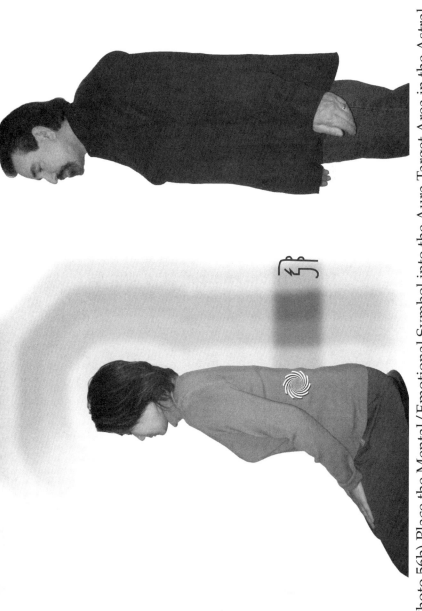

(Photo 56b) Place the Mental/Emotional Symbol into the Aura Target Area in the Astral Layer that is aligned with the second Chakra.

The firm, the enduring, the simple, and the modest are near to virtue.

-Confucius

Reiki Aura Attunement
Shame

thirty
three

Intent

If the exact mental or emotional issue is known, use Root Intent, if not known, use Generic Intent.

1. You have prepared for the Aura Attunement.

2. You are in the proper position to either perform the Attunement on yourself or another person in a quiet area where you will not be disturbed.

3. State the intent for the Aura Attunement silently to yourself before you begin. At this time, you can also ask for guidance during the Attunement. *Step should only take a few seconds.*

4. If you are a Reiki Master, place the Master Symbol into the palms of your hands, then activate it. **2nd Level Healers omit this step.**

5. Now place the Power Symbol into the palms of your hands and activate it.

6. Next place the Mental/Emotional Symbol into the Aura Target Area in the Astral Layer that is aligned with the second Chakra as shown (Photos 57 and 57b), then activate the symbol. *Step should only take 15 seconds.*

7. Now channel Reiki directly into the Aura Target Area about one to two inches away from where you have placed the Mental/Emotional Symbol. Do this with focus and the intent you have decided upon. *Step should only take about 2 minutes.*

8. Next, place the Mental/Emotional Symbol into the second Aura Target Area in the Astral Layer that is aligned with the seventh Chakra as shown (Photos 58 and 58b), then activate the symbol. *Step should only take 15 seconds.*

9. Now channel Reiki directly into the Aura Target Area about one to two inches away from where you have placed the Mental/Emotional Symbol. Do this with focus and the intent you have decided upon. *Step should only take about 2 minutes.*

10. The Attunement is complete. Perform the finishing steps.

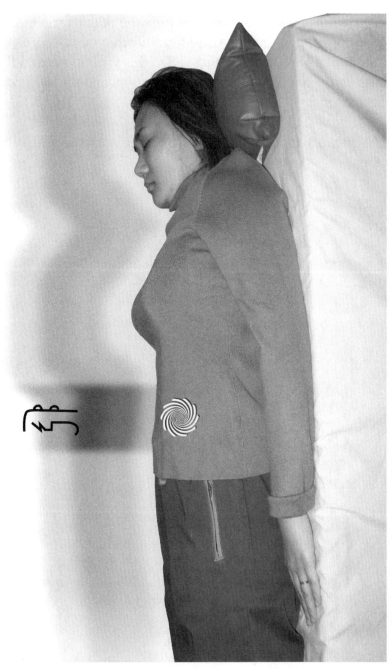

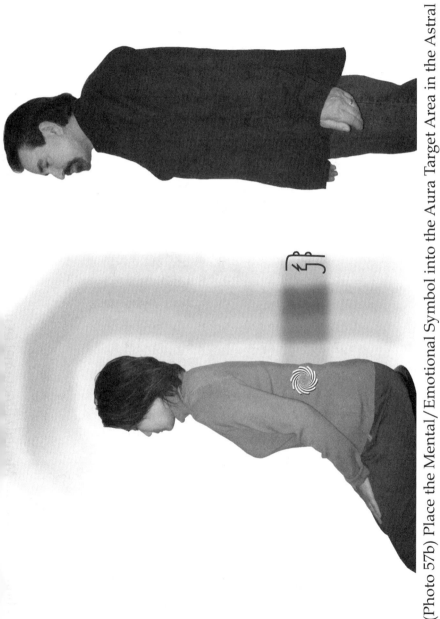

(Photo 57b) Place the Mental/Emotional Symbol into the Aura Target Area in the Astral Layer that is aligned with the second Chakra.

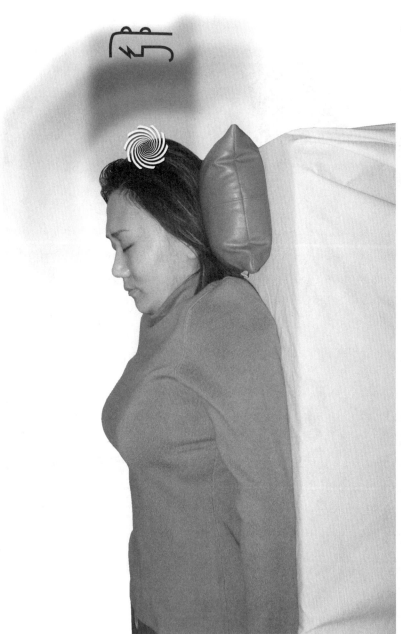

(Photo 58) Place the Mental/Emotional Symbol into the Aura Target Area in the Astral

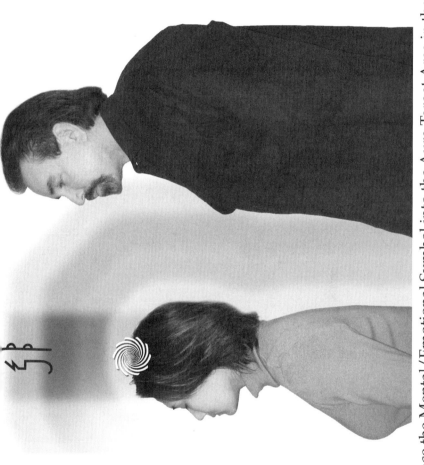

(Photo 58b) Place the Mental/Emotional Symbol into the Aura Target Area in the Astral Layer that is aligned with the seventh Chakra.

313

When anger rises, think of the consequences.
-Confucius

Reiki Aura Attunement
Spiritual Issues

thirty four

Intent

If the exact mental or emotional spiritual issue is known, use Root Intent, but if not known, use Generic Intent.

1. You have prepared for the Aura Attunement.

2. You are in the proper position to either perform the Attunement on yourself or another person in a quiet area where you will not be disturbed.

3. State the intent for the Aura Attunement silently to yourself before you begin. At this time, you can also ask for guidance during the Attunement. *Step should only take a few seconds.*

4. If you are a Reiki Master, place the Master Symbol into the palms of your hands, then activate it. **2nd Level Healers omit this step.**

5. Now place the Power Symbol into the palms of your hands and activate it.

6. Next place the Mental/Emotional Symbol into the Aura Target Area in the Astral Layer that is aligned with the seventh Chakra as shown (Photos 59 and 59b), then activate the symbol. *Step should only take 15 seconds.*

7. Now channel Reiki directly into the Aura Target Area about one to two inches away from where you have placed the Mental/Emotional Symbol. Do this with focus and the intent you have decided upon. *Step should only take about 2 minutes.*

8. Next, place the Mental/Emotional Symbol into the second Aura Target Area in the Astral Layer that is aligned with the fifth Chakra as shown (Photos 60 and 60b), then activate the symbol. *Step should only take 15 seconds.*

9. Now channel Reiki directly into the Aura Target Area about one to two inches away from where you have placed the Mental/Emotional Symbol. Do this with focus and the intent you have decided upon. *Step should only take about 2 minutes.*

10. The Attunement is complete. Perform the finishing steps.

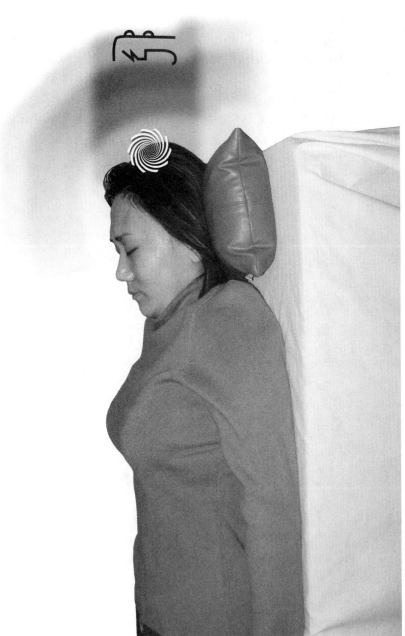

(Photo 59)Place the Mental / Emotional Symbol into the Aura Target Area in the Astral

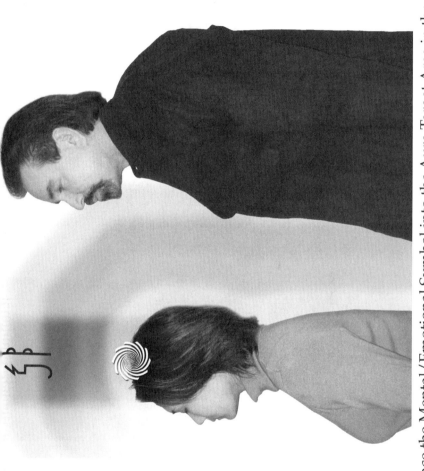

(Photo 59b) Place the Mental/Emotional Symbol into the Aura Target Area in the Astral Layer that is aligned with the seventh Chakra.

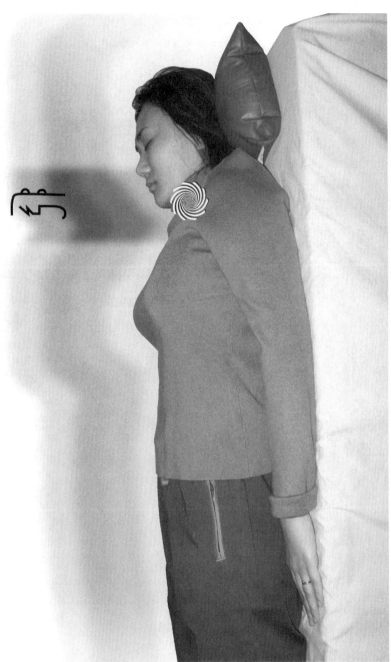

(Photo 60) Place the Mental/Emotional Symbol into the Aura Target Area in the Astral

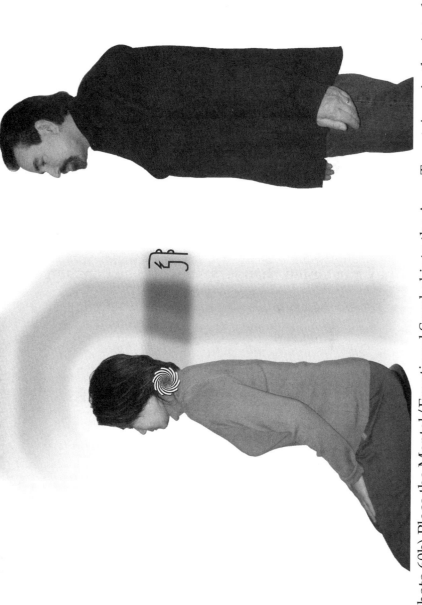

(Photo 60b) Place the Mental/Emotional Symbol into the Aura Target Area in the Astral Layer that is aligned with the fifth Chakra.

They must often change, who would be constant in happiness or wisdom.

-Confucius

Reiki Aura Attunement
Weight Issues

thirty five

Intent

It is difficult to use Root Intent for this Attunement because the majority of the time there are several mental or emotional issues that have mainfested and they are not easily uncovered. Just use Generic Intent for this Attunement, but if you know the Root Intent, by all means use it.

1. You have prepared for the Aura Attunement.

2. You are in the proper position to either perform the Attunement on yourself or another person in a quiet area where you will not be disturbed.

3. State the intent for the Aura Attunement silently to yourself before you begin. At this time, you can also ask for guidance during the Attunement. *Step should only take a few seconds.*

4. If you are a Reiki Master, place the Master Symbol into the palms of your hands, then activate it. *2nd Level Healers omit this step.*

5. Now place the Power Symbol into the palms of your hands and activate it.

6. Next place the Mental/Emotional Symbol into the Aura Target Area in the Astral Layer that is aligned with the first Chakra as shown (Photos 61 and 61b), then activate the symbol. *Step should only take 15 seconds.*

7. Now channel Reiki directly into the Aura Target Area about one to two inches away from where you have placed the Mental/Emotional Symbol. Do this with focus and the intent you have decided upon. *Step should only take about 2 minutes.*

8. Next, place the Mental/Emotional Symbol into the second Aura Target Area in the Astral Layer that is aligned with the second Chakra as shown (Photos 62 and 62b), then activate the symbol. *Step should only take 15 seconds.*

9. Now channel Reiki directly into the Aura Target Area about one to two inches away from where you have placed the Mental/Emotional Symbol. Do this with focus and the intent you have decided upon. *Step should only take about 2 minutes.*

10. The Attunement is complete. Perform the finishing steps.

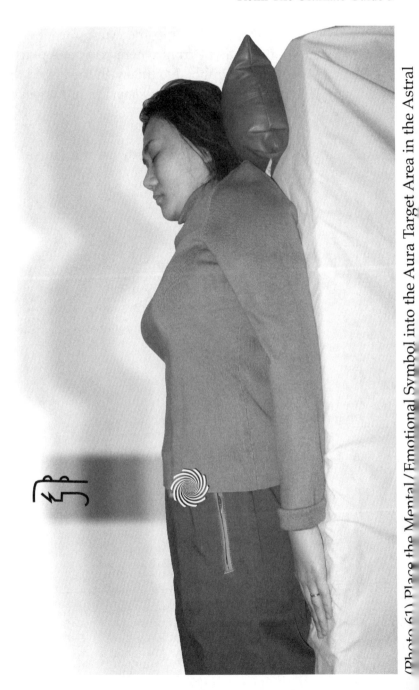

(Photo 61) Place the Mental/Emotional Symbol into the Aura Target Area in the Astral

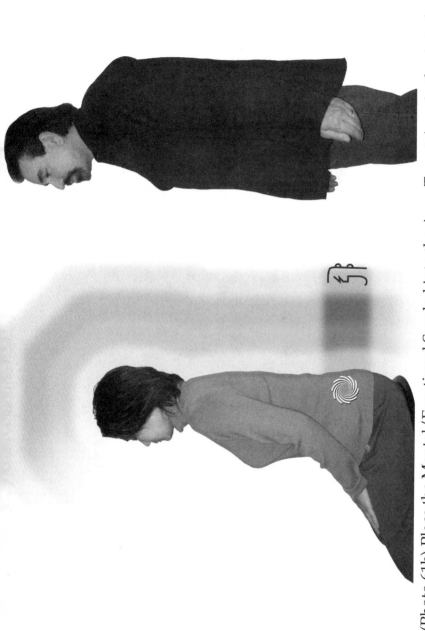

(Photo 61b) Place the Mental/Emotional Symbol into the Aura Target Area in the Astral Layer that is aligned with the first Chakra.

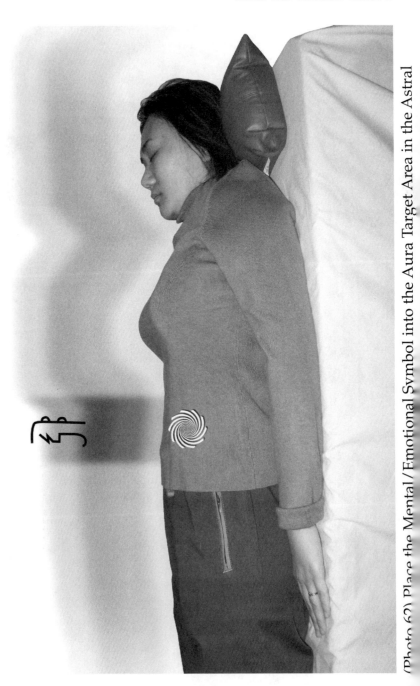

(Photo 62) Place the Mental / Emotional Symbol into the Aura Target Area in the Astral

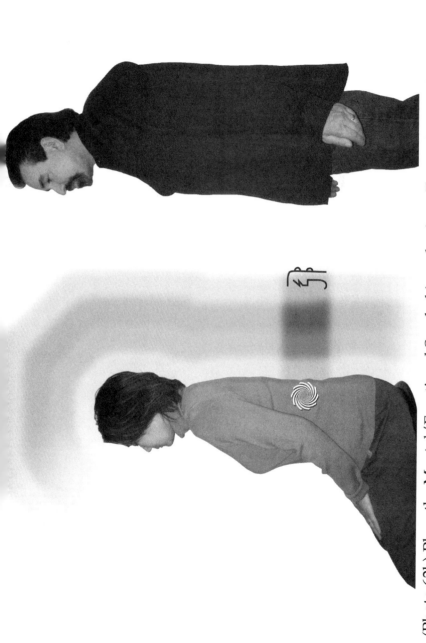

(Photo 62b) Place the Mental/Emotional Symbol into the Aura Target Area in the Astral Layer that is aligned with the second Chakra.

329

Shanti
Steve Murray

330

Shanti
Steve Murray

Aura Colors Interpretations

Here are some simple, basic common interpretations of the colors most frequently seen in the Aura. They are intended to be guides if you desire to develop your own skills in reading an Aura's color.

Keep in mind there are different interpretations or combined interpretations depending on the shade and the clarity or brightness of the color in the Aura. Sound and light frequencies and a person's unique physical, emotional, mental, and spiritual state can affect the Aura's color. Add to this the fact that not every person perceives colors the same; therefore, you can understand why any and all charts like this are only guides and can be very subjective.

Black
- ◆ Hatred – Negativity – Depression

Blue
- ◆ Spirituality – Pride – Adoration – Dedication

Brown
- ◆ Selfishness – Deception – Confusion Discouragement

Green
- ◆ Healed – Healing

Gold
- ◆ Spiritually Developed

Orange
- ◆ Confidence – Ambition – Pride – Self-sufficiency, Success

Pink
- ◆ Love – Affection – Enjoyment – Resilience

Purple
- ◆ Spiritual Awareness – Self-esteem – High ideals

Red
- ◆ Fear – Anger – Violent – Selfish – Deceitful

White
- ◆ Purity – Protection

Yellow
- ◆ Intelligence – Wisdom – Success – Creativeness

Reiki Symbols

The Reiki Symbols that I use during the Reiki Aura Attunements are the classic Usui Symbols and the truest from the Usui lineage. There are only minor variations with these Reiki Symbols when they are traced from this lineage.

There are other symbols that a few Reiki Masters and schools are using and teaching, but they are not a part of the Usui System. These symbols have been developed and created by different Reiki schools and Reiki Masters.

Variations of the Symbols

If you discover the Reiki Symbols you have been taught and to which you have been attuned vary from the ones in this book, do not worry about it, you still received a Reiki Attunement. This can include Reiki Symbols with different lines, extra lines, and lines that go in reverse directions. The symbols you received from your Reiki Master are the right symbols for you to use because you have been attuned to them. What is important is activating and using the Reiki Symbols to which you have been attuned.

There are a few reasons for the variations of the Reiki Symbols. In the past, Reiki Symbols were taught orally. Students were not allowed to write them down for hundreds of years, so when it was time for students to teach the Reiki symbols, they taught them orally, from memory. That is not the best system in terms of accuracy, so variations in the symbols developed. Now, most of the time, Reiki Symbols are written on paper, which keeps variations to a minimum.

Another recent reason for variations of the symbols is that some Reiki Masters have intentionally changed the Reiki Symbols. They have done this to make their Reiki unique, personal, and to blend with their current beliefs, or they have been told by their Reiki guides to make the changes.

Translation of the Symbols

I have seen many different translations and interpretations of the Reiki Symbols. I believe the following are the most traditional and accepted ones. Translations and interpretations are tough, especially when derived from several languages. The Bible is a prime example because it has been translated into many languages from its original, resulting in some discrepancies between some original parts of the Bible and the translations.

Feel free to use an interpretation that you were taught. Just be aware and open to other (i.e., different) interpretations. There is no right or wrong, it's just a matter of where you got your information.

Cho Ku Rei

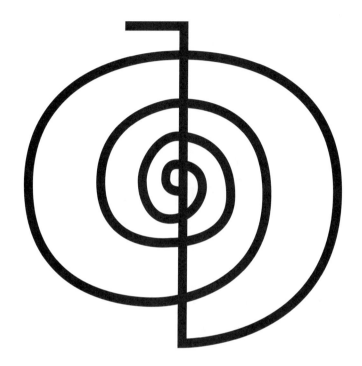

This is the Usui Power Symbol. It is also called the "Power Increase Symbol." Its name is Cho Ku Rei. The name of the Power Symbol means, "Put all the power in the universe here." The Power Symbol has many uses when activated, but it is primarily used to increase the power of Reiki or to focus Reiki on a specific location and for protection.

Sei He Ki

This is the Usui Mental/Emotional Symbol. It is also called the "Emotional/Mental Symbol," the "Mental Symbol," or the "Mental/Emotional/Addiction Symbol." Its name is Sei He Ki. The name of this symbol means, "God and humanity become One." This symbol has many uses when activated, but is commonly used in emotional, mental, and addictive healing situations.

Hon Sha Ze Sho Nen

This is the Usui Long Distance symbol. It is also called the "Long Distance and the Absentee Symbol." Its name is Hon Sha Ze Sho Nen. The name of this symbol has a few different interpretations. I was taught that it means, "May the Buddha in me connect to the Buddha in you to promote harmony and peace." The symbol is very powerful and flexible and most healers do not utilize its full ability. When activated with specific intent, Reiki can be sent anywhere, anytime in the past, present, or future. Distance, time, and space are not a barrier when you use this symbol.

Dai Koo Myo

This is the Reiki Usui Master Symbol. Its name is Dai Koo Myo. With this symbol, there are also several translations, but the one I use is, "Great Being of the universe shine on me, be my friend." The Master Symbol is the ultimate Reiki Symbol in all aspects. It intensifies Reiki, takes it to a higher level, and creates a stronger connection with your source. When you activate other Reiki Symbols with the Master Symbol, the symbols are then taken to their highest level of effectiveness.

Index

Selected Bibliography

Andrews, T., (2002). *How To See & Read the Aura*. Llewellyn Publications. [ISBN 0-875420133]

Bain, G.H., (1998). *Auras 101: A Basic Study of Human Auras and the Techniques to See Them*. Light Technology Publications. [ISBN 1-891824074]

Bowers, B., (December 15, 1989). *What Color is Your Aura?* Pocket. [ISBN 0-671707639]

Cayce, E., (1973). *Auras: An Essay on the Meaning of Colors*. A.R.E. Press. [ISBN 0-876040121]

Martin, B., Moraitis, D., (2003). *Change Your Aura, Change Your Life*. Spiritual Arts Institute. [ISBN 0-970211813]

McLaren, K., (1998). *Your Aura & Your Chakras: The Owner's Manual*. Weiser Books. [ISBN 1-578630479]

Rosetree, R., (2004). *Aura Reading Through ALL Your Senses*. Women's Intuition Worldwide. [ISBN 0-965114546]

Slate, J., (1999). *Aura Energy For Health, Healing & Balance*. Llewellyn Publications. [ISBN 1-567186378]

Smith, M., (2002). *Auras*. Llewellyn Publications. [ISBN 1-567186432]

Sugiyama, S., (2002). *Aura, Ki, and Healing*. Shojiro Sugiyama [ISBN 0-966904842]

Webster, R., (1951). *Aura Reading For Beginners*. Llewellyn Publications. [ISBN 1-567187986]

HOW TO ORDER , DVDS, CDs, BOOKS

To buy any of the following Books, DVDs or CDs, check with your local bookstore, or www.healingreiki.com, or email bodymindheal@aol.com, or call 949-263-4676

DVDs-CDs-BOOKS

BOOKS BY STEVE MURRAY

Reiki The Ultimate Guide
Learn Sacred Symbols and Attunements
Plus Reiki Secrets You Should Know

Reiki The Ultimate Guide Vol. 2
Learn Reiki Healing with Chakras
plus New Reiki Healing Attunements
for All Levels

Reiki The Ultimate Guide Vol. 3
Learn New Reiki Aura Attunements
Heal Mental and Emotional Issues

Cancer Guided Imagery Program
For Radiation, Chemotherapy, Surgery
and Recovery

Stop Eating Junk!
In 5 Minutes a Day for 21 Days

DVDS BY STEVE MURRAY

Reiki Master Attunement
Become a Reiki Master

Reiki 1st Level Attunement
Give Healing Energy to Yourself
and Others

Reiki 2nd Level Attunement
Learn and Use the Reiki Sacred
Symbols

Reiki Psychic Attunement
Open and Expand Your Psychic
Abilities

Reiki Healing Attunement
Heal Emotional-Mental Physical-
Spiritual Issues

Lose Fat and Weight
Stop Eating Junk!
In 5 Minutes a Day for 21 Days

Cancer Guided Imagery
Program for Radiation

Cancer Guided Imagery
Program for Chemotherapy

Cancer Guided Imagery
Program for Surgery

30-Day Subliminal
Weight Loss Program

Pain Relief Using Your
Unconscious Mind
A Subliminal Program

Fear & Stress Relief
Using Your Unconscious Mind
A Subliminal Program

Stop Smoking Using Your
Unconscious Mind
A Subliminal Program

CDs BY STEVE MURRAY

Reiki Healing Music
Attunement: Volume One

Reiki Healing Music
Attunement: Volume Two

Reiki Psychic Music
Attunement: Volume One

Reiki Psychic Music
Attunement: Volume Two

Cancer Fear & Stress Relief Program
Reduce Fear and Stress During Cancer
Treatment and Recovery

DVDs BY BODY & MIND PRODUCTIONS

Learning to Read the Tarot
Intuitively

Learning to Read the Symbolism
of the Tarot

More of what people are saying...

I am a Reiki Master and I was taught the secretive way of Reiki. However, I must admit, I admire and appreciate Steve Murray's approach to teaching Reiki. Steve's new book Reiki the Ultimate Guide Vol. 2 is excellent. I learned things I never knew and am most grateful for the education. Steve is a "way shower" and his new book was quite enlightening for me. This book is at the heart of "true Reiki." If you are interested in helping others and yourself to heal, this book is a must. *DS*

Steve Murray has my eternal gratitude for sharing his personal journey with Reiki Mastership and the battles he fought and has ultimately won. His book is a fabulous Reiki guide and is easy to read, comprehend, and is one of the most informative, down-to-earth books out there on the subject today. It is filled with essential information covering every aspect of Reiki and more. I admire him greatly for his courage and for being a beacon of light in this universe. Reiki is a gift to be shared and Steve has accomplished this with truth and integrity. *GS*

I have never come across guides like this! It is a "must have" for any level Reiki Practitioner. Steve Murray truly takes the time to guide you through the Reiki process. It is a wonderful guide for both beginners to Reiki and Masters as well. *JM*

Steve Murray clearly stands by his vow, stated in his book, THE ULTIMATE GUIDE TO REIKI, and he brings clarity, integrity, simplicity, and freedom to Reiki and those desirous of learning it. Steve has written the Reiki Bible, in my opinion, I highly recommend THE ULTIMATE GUIDE TO REIKI. *NG*

Steve Murray has an excellent talent for simplifying and clarifying what can be an intensely abstract and complex topic, making the material easily understood and assimilated by the neophyte. His delivery comes from a practical, straightforward standpoint--with neither the egotistical elitism, nor the control freak power grip that sadly seems to plague this field.*SM*

I have recently received both my Reiki Psychic Attunement and Reiki Master Attunement from Steve Murray via DVD. These, along with Steve's Reiki the Ultimate Guide (both I and II) have truly opened up many new awarenesses and experiences for me. I have already had the chance to help several friends and family members using the Reiki healing programs. Steve Murray's programs have answered all my questions and are continuing to help me in my Reiki journey. *SZ*

As a Teaching Reiki Master, I have a huge library of Reiki literature and have read many books. This one book was the best I have found in my 30 years of work on my path to the light. I will use it as a teaching resource with my students and encourage them to purchase it as a guide. The attunement videos are exquisite! In my viewing of them I experienced energy and colors like none I have felt before. *KW*

This book is terrific! I recently had a client whose chakras would not stay balanced. After reading Steve's book, I tried his solution and had immediate success. Thanks, Steve, for another wonderful book! I find Steve's book to be clear and well written. The photos are especially informative and easy to understand. *CM*

Steve Murray's Reiki The Ultimate Guide Vol. 2, far exceeded my already great expectations. With the same easy-to-read-and-understand methods used in the first book, he goes into brand new territory. With concise pictures and easy-to-follow directions, Mr. Murray teaches the Reiki Practitioner how to take what they know and utilize it in a far more advanced and practical way to treat physical ailments. His coverage of Chakras and Meridians is important for any Reiki healer to know. I used the new healing attunement method to treat someone and achieved great success in my first attempt. It was simple, yet brilliant! *FK*

The Ultimate Guide and his Attunement program comes with my highest recommendation. Murray delivered what he promised and I was able to obtain tangible results very quickly. All of Murray's materials have been money well spent. This has truly changed me, at a very fundamental level. *HJW*

About the Author

Steve Murray is the author of the best selling *Reiki The Ultimate Guide* trilogy and has a series of self-healing programs on DVD. The DVD subjects include Reiki Attunements, Cancer Guided Imagery, weight loss, pain, fear and stress relief to name just a few. He has produced four Reiki CDs for healing, meditation, and psychic work.

Steve is an experienced Usui Reiki Master, Tibetan and Karuna Reiki® Master. One of his most powerful Attunements came from the High Priest of the Essene Church, which made him an Essene Healer. The Essenes have been healers for more than 2,000 years. Steve is also a Hypnotherapist and a member of the National League of Medical Hypnotherapists and National Guild of Hypnotists.